KYOTO

SEVEN PATHS TO THE HEART OF THE CITY

DIANE DURSTON

Photography by KATSUHIKO MIZUNO

KODANSHA INTERNATIONAL
Tokyo • New York • London

PAGE 1
A mist lingers over the Togetsu-kyo Bridge in Sagano Toriimoto.

PAGE 2–3
One of the many cobbled paths in Kyoto. This one, in the geisha quarter of Gion, leads to the elegant restaurant Umemura.

PAGE 3
The Moon Float (*tsuki hoko*) in the annual Gion Festival passes through a Kyoto neighborhood.

ENDPAPERS
A scene from the Edo-period screen painting, *Gion Festival*.

ON-SITE EDITOR IN KYOTO: JOSEPH CRONIN
INTERIOR MAPS: NORIKO MUROTANI
KYOTO CITY MAP: TADAMITSU OMORI
CALLIGRAPHY: KENHO UI

NOTE: *Japanese names in the body of the text are given in the traditional Japanese order, surname before given name.*

Distributed in the United States by Kodansha America, Inc., 575 Lexington Avenue, New York, N.Y. 10022, and in the United Kingdom and continental Europe by Kodansha Europe Ltd., 95 Aldwych, London WC2B 4JF. Published by Kodansha International Ltd., 17–14 Otowa 1-chome, Bunkyoku, Tokyo 112-8652, and Kodansha America, Inc.

First edition, 2002
01 02 03 04 05   5 4 3 2 1

www.thejapanpage.com

CONTENTS

PREFACE

"To search the old is to find the new."
—Confucius

The dawn never "breaks" in Kyoto—it wouldn't dare. It proceeds cautiously down the Eastern Mountains with all due respect, taking pains not to awaken the sleepy twelve-hundred-year-old princess too roughly from her courtly dreams. The sun forgets at moments like this that all the princesses have gone.

Dawn in Kyoto is a time of great beauty. The restless old women rise first, rustling about with their potted plants and laundry poles, dousing the pavement at their doorsteps with water from tin ladles, making fresh the stage for this new day's busyness.

A cavernous bronze temple bell echoes hauntingly in tones so somber that only old men with no further use for alarm clocks awaken to its distant toll. Portly ex-soldiers stretch and wheeze before their bonsai shelves, shuffling gruffly off down the alley with offerings for the neighborhood shrine (their two resounding claps required to rouse the slumbering deities disturbing night-owl students and sleepless writers in the process). Still in his long cotton pajamas, the balding old gentleman considers this narrow street nothing but a broader definition of "home." At 7 A.M., there is still an hour or so of calm left till the twenty-first century sets in again.

The best time to see Kyoto is early in the morning—before anyone else does. Wander the old neighborhoods while the ambiguous light still blurs the concrete edges, softens the amplified voices, and slows the pulse of the modern city. This is the hour that brings back the legend and spirit of "the ancient capital of Japan."

Tatsumibashi Bridge over the Shirakawa river is a favorite spot to catch *maiko* hurrying along to their next engagement in the heart of the Gion district.

M A C H I N A M I

The Forgotten Treasures of Kyoto

The smaller of two gardens (*tsubo niwa*) of Gen'an House, a *machiya* in Nishijin.

"The quality we call beauty must always grow from the realities of life, and our ancestors, forced to live in dark rooms, presently came to discover the beauty in shadows, ultimately to guide shadows to beauty's end. And so it has come to be that the beauty of a Japanese room depends on a variation of shadows, heavy shadows against light shadows . . . it has nothing else." —Tanizaki Jun'ichiro

THERE ARE PLACES left in Kyoto, outside the grand temple gates and villa walls, where the way of life of the everyday townspeople goes on as if the modern circus had yet to come to town. And as with ancient cities the world over, blind alleys and old women tell the best stories.

Down every back street in Kyoto are remnants of a way of life that is rapidly disappearing. Vignettes from the past cling to niches and alleyways here and there throughout the city. But the economic and social upheavals that have taken place since the end of World War II have left their mark on the classic old neighborhoods of wooden rowhouses, the *machinami* of Kyoto. Today only a handful of these neighborhoods remain intact. Throughout most of the city, traditional houses are now wedged like aching teeth between their shiny new concrete and stucco neighbors.

This book leads you through seven districts in which echoes of the old *machinami* linger—past the traditional homes, the old shops and inns, and the tiny neighborhood shrines that line these narrow old streets in the heart of the city. Four of these seven areas are now preserved by law; the other three are partially protected, but have yet to be saved from the bulldozers that will almost inevitably take them.

THE HISTORY OF THE *MACHINAMI* OF KYOTO

To learn something of the history of the *machinami* is to discover much about the history of Kyoto itself—and because Kyoto was the capital of Japan for over ten centuries—of the development of Japan as a whole, historically, culturally, and economically. The values of the merchant class that developed in these Kyoto neighborhoods during the middle ages were the basis for the modern economic success to which Japan would one day rise.

The term *machinami* describes the rows of wooden houses (or *machiya*) that line the narrow streets of these old neighborhoods. Groups of approximately forty *machiya* are collectively known as *cho*, and residents refer to their *o-cho-nai* (honorable inner town), the primary social and political unit to which they belong. In Kyoto, almost everything is deemed "honorable," from neighborhoods (*o-cho-nai*) to monkeys (*o-saru-san*) and almost everything between—hence the constant use of the prefix "*o*."

An even smaller social unit exists within the *cho*: the five-family unit that has been known for centuries as the *gonin-gumi*. Historically,

each family in one of these groups was directly responsible for its actions to the two families on either side whose walls often adjoined their own, as well as to the two families whose homes faced them across the narrow street. The *gonin-gumi* system is credited indirectly with much of the responsibility for the safety of Kyoto's streets. A crime committed by a member of one family reflected on the other four. In centuries past, punishment was meted out not only to individuals but to the whole *gumi*. In effect, neighborhoods still police themselves in many ways, holding each other answerable for their actions, based on this sense of mutual responsibility.

KYO-MACHIYA

The smallest neighborhood unit in Kyoto was the traditional family dwelling, the *machiya*, or town house. Because of the long narrow shape of these wooden rowhouses, the local people jokingly refer to them as *unagi no nedoko*—the bedrooms of eels. As the dwellings were only 8 meters (26 feet) wide, but over 40 meters (130 feet) long, the nickname was well deserved.

Every *Kyo-machiya*, or Kyoto town house, is constructed from a single architectural standard of measurement, the size of a single tatami mat—roughly 1 by 2 meters (3 by 6 feet) square. Rooms are measured according to the number of mats they contain, which then determines the width and length of every house. This modular system

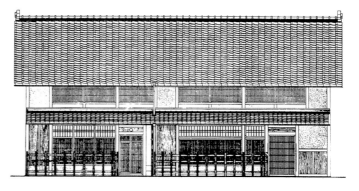

Two *Kyo-machiya* share walls and a roof, a common characteristic of homes in the *machinami* neighborhoods. Note the separate entrance that defines each dwelling.

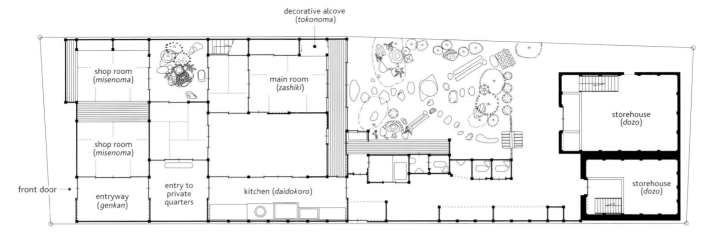

The floor plan of this *machiya* shows the long narrow shape of these urban dwellings. The shop room was at the front of the house, the family quarters were at the back, with a long narrow kitchen in the middle. The two small gardens indicate that this was the home of an affluent merchant family.

of measurement allowed for interchangeable features, including sliding doors. This also meant that not only the individual house but the proportions of the entire neighborhood could be traced back to this one small unit of measure, making the *machiya* unique in the world of architecture.

The façade of a typical *Kyo-machiya* has certain interesting design features. The *inuyarai*, a curved bamboo cover over the gutter in front of each house (literally, a "dog barrier"), was used as a buffer to keep pests, even the two-legged kind, at a distance from dwellings that opened right onto the street. Some of the *machiya* still have a *komayose*, the now decorative wooden railing that was used originally as a hitching post in the days when horses were the only means of transportation in Kyoto. In fact, many of Kyoto's side streets were not paved until after World War II.

The somber façade of a typical *Kyo-machiya* often seems forbidding as you approach from the street. The dark slatted windows called *koshimado* shielded residents from the eyes of passersby, a means of creating privacy amid the bustle of city life that goes on outside, just inches away. In some types of *machiya*, removable front storm doors could be opened up to reveal the room nearest the street called the *misenoma*, the shop room. Having the shop right on the street and the living quarters tucked behind afforded the owners the convenience of being able to work at home. Older residents of Kyoto neighborhoods reminisce about the days when children used to watch craftsmen work in their open shop fronts, a practice no longer followed.

Customers enter the sliding door in front and step into the *toriniwa*, a breezeway that leads back through the kitchen all the way to the interior of the house. The *noren* curtain hung in place over the entry is an indication that the shop is open for business. Another curtain, often a *nawa noren*, or rope curtain, separates the kitchen from the shop front. Stepping up from the *toriniwa* to the raised tatami shop room, customers sit down to discuss business over a cup of green tea with the proprietor. Customs like this continue in modern Japanese business. A cup of green tea still awaits anyone doing business in corporate headquarters all over Japan.

Except for the *toriniwa*, which often had a dirt or stone floor, all the rooms of the *machiya* were raised approximately 60 centimeters (2 feet) above ground level to provide adequate ventilation during Kyoto's humid summers. Every *machiya* in Kyoto is designed with the idea of keeping cool in the summer. Though the winters are cold, it is easier to bundle up than to endure the heat and humidity, which some-

times lasts for four or five months. The use of woven tatami mats as flooring material throughout is said to allow the floor to "breathe." The sliding paper doors (*fusuma*) act as room dividers that can be removed to adapt the space for various uses. These paper doors are replaced with reed screens during the summer months to help ventilation or, to create as much of a breeze as possible, are removed completely.

The ancient division of the city into a tidy grid pattern by Emperor Kanmu over twelve hundred years ago determined the long, narrow subdivision of lots within each city block—that and the fact that taxes were once levied based on the amount of street frontage each dwelling possessed.

Unlike the more spacious homes of the privileged samurai, where a small garden separated the entrance from the street, *machiya* gardens, or *tsubo niwa*, were a private, limited space located deep in the interior—always a refreshing surprise. Here the master of the house could create a small paradise all his own. *Tsubo niwa* refers to the tiny size of these interior light wells, one *tsubo* being a land measurement that equals the size of two tatami mats. Some of Kyoto's most exquisite gardens are not more than 2 meters (6 feet) square.

The homes of prosperous merchants often had more than one interior garden, one of which acted as a divider between the *misenoma* and the living quarters in the back. Polished wood verandahs ran along the edges of these interior gardens, linking inside and out. The deep

eaves make this a fine location for contemplating the harvest moon in comfort, protected from an unexpected evening shower.

The *zashiki* is the heart of the house. It is used as a space for entertaining guests, though the function of rooms in a *machiya* can change in a moment with the removal of the *fusuma* doors that serve as walls. This makes for a flexible environment, a necessity in houses in which there were often only two rooms for every possible family activity.

The *zashiki* is the most elegantly designed room in the house. Facing the *oku niwa*, or rear garden, the *zashiki* more than any other space in the home shows the influence of the tea ceremony on *machiya*. Like the traditional tea room, the *zashiki* has a *tokonoma*, the recessed niche of honor where a single scroll painting and a flower arrangement are the only embellishments in the shadowy interior of the house.

Apart from the *zashiki*, one of the most impressive rooms is, not surprisingly, the kitchen, the heart of every home. The ceiling of this room features massive curved beams that support the heavy tile roof exposed to view. Light streams down through the skylights, and an old well, no longer in use, sits in one corner, while a large clay oven, the *kamado*, and its giant, clay rice caldron squat in the other. Near the oven is one of the very special features of the *machiya*, one that is really its "soul." No *machiya* kitchen would be without a tiny shrine to the god of fire. The roots of ancient Japanese culture are founded in the deeply felt tradition of paying respect to the *kami*, or gods, who protect everything from ovens to rice fields. Not to be meddled with, the *kami* are sure to receive their daily due of flowers and votive candles, to keep the household safe from fires. Kyoto was destroyed by fires many times over its long history, and no household would be without a symbolic bucket of water, replenished daily by the lady of the house as a reminder that one must take special care with fire in these wooden neighborhoods, many of which share walls.

In days past, dry goods and housewares were kept in long wooden cabinets called a *mizuya*, which lined one wall of every kitchen. Pickling, salt preservation, and drying were the only means available to housewives until the refrigerator came to Kyoto as late as the mid-1960s.

Behind the main garden at the back of the property in the homes of the most prosperous merchants was the *kura*, or family storehouse. The thick walls and heavy doors provided a place to keep the family treasures safe from fire and theft. Many merchants used their *kura* as warehouses to store goods for sale, since the small shop room in front usually provided only enough space to display samples and conduct business.

Historically, the small townships that these homes make up formed in self-defense against the constantly warring political factions that periodically left the city in ruin during the middle ages. Remnants of moats that were built by residents originally to defend their *cho* can still be found in some of the old neighborhoods.

The heart of the family life was the *kamado*, or kitchen hearth, where giant iron caldrons boiled the day's rice.

ARCHITECTURAL STYLES

Architectural styles differed in Kyoto, depending upon the profession of a particular neighborhood's inhabitants. Groups of craftsmen formed guilds in specific areas, forming whole districts of silk weavers, dyers, or potters.

The architectural style of a particular *cho* was determined by the requirements of the group's trade and its proximity to a shrine or temple. The sense of community within a township was demonstrated in the unified style of elements like the type of roof tiles, the depth of the eaves, and in the pattern and number of slats in the window grates.

It was a breach of propriety to flaunt one's personal wealth by outdoing your neighbors in the adornment of a façade, so the prosperous merchant displayed his success with lavish touches to the interior: hand-carved transoms, lacquered trims, the use of elaborately decorated paper on sliding *fusuma* doors, and so on.

However, tact and good taste were not the only considerations determining the restrained exteriors of the homes of Kyoto merchants. Strictly enforced edicts were issued by the shogunate during the Edo period (1600–1868) forbidding any extravagant displays in the merchants' houses, inside or outside, in an attempt to keep members of the rising merchant class in their lowly place at the bottom of the social class system. One example of the stringent laws of this period is that no merchant was allowed to build a house over two stories high. By the middle of the Edo period, however, the merchants had achieved a powerful enough position financially to manifest their individual tastes, particularly in elements of interior design, regardless of the shogun and his edicts.

Another formidable enemy of the wooden *machiya* and its inhabitants was fire, as mentioned earlier. The long history of Kyoto reads like a list of regularly scheduled conflagrations. The Great Tenmei Fire in 1788 destroyed nearly eighty percent of the city. For this reason, virtually no residential structure dating before that time remains standing in central Kyoto.

One positive aspect of this repeated destruction and rebuilding is that the people banded together within their communities. Each neighborhood developed its own special customs, rules, and architectural features that symbolized the unity of the townspeople within them. As much as the architectural beauty of the old *machinami* neighborhoods, it is this spirit of unity within them that is what historic preservationists in Kyoto today seek to keep alive.

Many of the older *machiya* in Kyoto were built around the turn of the century, when horses were tied to the *komayose* wooden railings that protected the front of the house.

THE HISTORIC PRESERVATION MOVEMENT IN KYOTO

Efforts at historic preservation have been undertaken by the Japanese government, but most of the legislation that exists has been directed at monumental structures—at the castles, temples, shrines, and villas that still grace the landscape. For most historical cities of the world, historic preservation is a costly and painstaking endeavor. Kyoto, a city once built entirely of wood, has its hands full now with the restoration and maintenance of over two thousand wooden temples, shrines, and villas.

Because Kyoto was spared the bombings of World War II, however, the preservation not only of temples and shrines but of the traditional cityscape itself has taken on special historical significance. The wooden dwellings that remain in Kyoto are nearly all that is left of prewar urban Japan.

Preservationist stirrings were first felt in Japan as early as the Meiji period (1868–1912). The first conservation laws in Kyoto were passed in an effort to preserve scenic areas in the foothills of the mountains that surround the city on three sides. Since the passing of this first law over fifty years ago, construction has been largely prohibited on the hillsides, preserving for Kyoto the beautifully forested backdrop that these hills still provide.

In 1966, the Japanese government passed a law aimed at the preservation of historic areas in and around former capital cities. To date, approximately 60 square kilometers of historically important landscape have been set aside (of which 15 have relatively strict development and preservation regulations). An additional 12,950 hectares of land were designated as zones of scenic beauty.

For years, emphasis was on the historic and scenic areas in the foothills surrounding Kyoto. The movement to preserve historically and culturally important residential areas in the heart of the city came from the citizens themselves, resulting in the enactment of the Kyoto Urban Landscape Ordinance of 1972. This provided for the protection of special areas within the city by establishing guidelines for the height and design of buildings in the downtown area. Unfortunately, these guidelines are vaguely stated and have proven rather toothless, as evidenced by the eclectic cityscape visible today.

In the mid-1970s, citizens' groups directed their attention specifically at the *machinami*. In 1976, the first such *machinami* neighborhood was officially designated on a national level as a Traditional Building Preservation District—the Sanneizaka district at the foot of Kiyomizu Temple in eastern Kyoto. This was followed by Gion Shinbashi (one of the most famous of Kyoto's old geisha quarters just east of the Kamogawa river), Sagano Toriimoto (a rural village at the foot of Atago Shrine in western Kyoto), and Kamigamo Shaké-machi (an area of homes belonging to the descendants of priests of Kamigamo Shrine).

From the start, the urban-preservation movement in Kyoto has placed emphasis on the preservation of entire quarters of the city, rather than individual buildings. The *machinami* concept is essential to preservation efforts in Kyoto because the basic structure of the city—both socially and architecturally—is one of interwoven, interdependent parts. A 2000 census counted nearly thirteen thousand people per square kilometer in central Kyoto. Densely populated for centuries, the city's back streets are all narrow, in some places barely wide enough for a single car to pass, resulting in a closeness that would no doubt be disastrous in societies where individuality is the first priority. The *machinami* districts of Kyoto are symbols of a way of life, evolving over the centuries, in which people have learned to survive in tight quarters harmoniously.

The difficulty, however, of preserving entire neighborhoods has presented Kyoto with a monumental task. Obtaining the cooperation of an entire community is the first challenge, a prospect considerably more difficult than approaching a single household. Moreover, finding an old neighborhood that has remained relatively intact is a problem for any twenty-first-century city, perhaps especially in Japan, where the main thrust of the whole society has been toward total modernization since the end of World War II.

Other than the four *machinami* neighborhoods that have already been designated as historic preservation districts in Kyoto, it appears unlikely that any other areas will be added in the future for several reasons.

Zoning laws are extremely flexible in Kyoto, due to the traditional combination of shops, homes, and cottage industries within the same area. Much of the city falls under a "mixed" system of overlapping zones that has resulted in large areas classed as residential-commercial-industrial zones. As long as "industry and commerce" meant cottage industries like weaving and pottery, requiring only two-story wooden structures, this system worked. But the economic changes that have taken place over the past fifty years brought problems of noise and air pollution—and the need to expand. With the high price of land in Kyoto, it is not surprising that many businesses choose to tear down their old wooden structures and rebuild three- or four-story concrete structures on the same long, narrow lots—resulting in the visual chaos that is evident today. The city government encourages businesses to relocate in the less expensive southern part of the city, though this, too, means the loss of the less-prosperous southern district *machinami*.

The approach to the preservation of the *machinami* districts in Kyoto has been to provide guidelines for renovations to ensure that they continue to thrive as living, working neighborhoods, rather than as museum pieces. With the help of architects at Kyoto University, residents now have access to historically accurate models for restorations within the four specially designated areas mentioned above. Exterior changes to buildings must conform to the architectural style of the preserved districts, but in order to accommodate the changing patterns of contemporary life, the owners are free to remodel the interior to suit present-day needs. This has resulted in the loss of the way of life the dwellings fostered, though the façades at least conform to the traditional style.

A few individual dwellings have become recognized as *bunkazai*, or cultural assets, a category that qualifies them for preservation assistance on a national level. In such cases, both interior and exterior must be preserved intact or meticulously restored to their original condition. Owners of these homes receive a part of the cost of renovation from the government, as do residents of preserved districts, but no tax allowances are made in either case. For that and various other reasons, many owners often decline government offers to have their homes honored with this title.

The current climate among much of the population of Kyoto for further modernization and for more individuality and freedom of expression is understandable—given the poverty and the repression of the past. While half the population is enthusiastic about saving the traditional character of Kyoto, the other half sees the old wooden dwellings as dinosaurs—anomalies that have outlived their time. In fact, so much has already been destroyed that the traditional image of Kyoto that tourists, both at home and abroad, have been led to expect is rapidly becoming more legend than reality.

If the preservationists were motivated simply by a nostalgic desire to cling to a past that seems more romantic in retrospect than it ever really was, developers could easily dismiss their attempts as sentimental and old-fashioned. More important than sentiment, however, is the principle of ensuring that the way of life to which these old neighborhoods gave shelter—the cooperation, the safety, the sense of pride—does not disappear with each old wooden home that ends in a pile of dust.

This *machiya* is known for its beautiful bamboo "*noren*" curtain. When the *noren* is hung out over the entrance to a shop, it is a symbol that the shop is open for business. The clay figure on the roof above the door is Shoki, the Demon Queller, a favorite guardian figure among Kyoto people, who collect and display a number of different traditional good-luck charms and amulets that they hope will protect their homes from misfortune. (Courtesy of the Arakawa family) ▶

SEVEN PATHS
TO THE HEART OF
THE CITY

"A leap from the stage at Kiyomizu" is a proverb used when one is willing to risk all to accomplish an impossible dream. The massive wooden platform is built entirely without nails, each interlocking post and beam was fitted into place by hand to construct this magnificent structure that supports the sweeping cedar rooftop of one of Kyoto's oldest and most famous Buddhist temples.

The finial of the five-storied Yasaka Pagoda, the spiritual center of its neighborhood for centuries, pierces the evening sky. ▶

S A N N E I Z A K A

All of us are pilgrims on this earth. I've even heard it said that the earth itself is a pilgrim in the heavens.

—Maxim Gorky, 1903

"PILGRIM"—A PERSON WHO TRAVELS a long distance to some sacred place; a traveler or wanderer. For over twelve centuries pilgrims have made their way up the steep cobblestone paths at the foot of the mountains in the east of Kyoto to Kiyomizu-dera temple. Founded in the eighth century, before Kyoto became the capital of Japan, this temple belongs to Everyman. Women come to pray to Kannon, the Goddess of Mercy, for an easy childbirth. Ascetics come to stand in midwinter under the icy waters of Otowa-no-taki to gain favor with the heavens. Young girls come to buy charms for luck in matters of love from Jishu Gongen, the shrine that adjoins Kiyomizu. For travelers, devotees, and school girls—this is Mecca in Japan.

The Sanneizaka district, named after one of the old cobbled streets that leads up the hill to Kiyomizu-dera, is a *monzencho*—a town that grew up outside the gates of a temple. Centuries ago, the shops along these streets catered to the needs of pilgrims, providing a cup of tea, a string of prayer beads, a memento of the journey and perhaps a bit of local advice on seeing the sights, the same as they do today.

Start your pilgrimage at Yasaka Jinja, the patron shrine of the Gion entertainment quarter in the area north and south of Shijo-dori avenue. Names on the lanterns at Yasaka Jinja are from local shops and teahouses in Gion where geisha entertain. There are any number of smaller shrines on these grounds, where famous kabuki actors from the nearby Minamiza Kabuki Theater came to pray for success on the stage.

Follow the path that leads from the south entrance to Yasaka Jinja—past clay-walled shrine grounds, half-hidden gardens, and private villas—to Ishibe-koji, a back street so narrow that in places they say you can touch both sides at once. The high stone walls that line this cobbled path lead through a maze of former villas turned teahouses and inns. The geisha of Gion entertain guests each evening behind reed-screen curtains in this exclusive, reclusive neighborhood—a quiet time-warp of a side trip on your way to Ninenzaka.

Kodai-ji temple perches on the hillside across the road from the entrance to Ishibe-koji. Here lived the widow of the famous sixteenth-century general Toyotomi Hideyoshi, retired to life in a regal nunnery built for her out of remorse by the shogun Tokugawa Ieyasu, the very man responsible for her husband's death.

Just south of Kodai-ji lies the Sanneizaka district, the first residential neighborhood to be officially designated a historic preservation district in Japan, in 1976. *Sannei* means "safe childbirth," referring to the belief that Kannon, the Goddess of Mercy, who is enshrined in Kiyomizu-dera, will protect any expectant mother who climbs the hill to pray here.

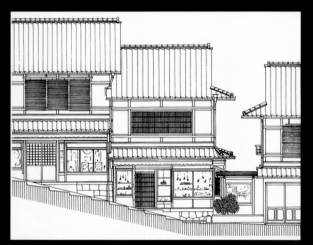

This illustration and photograph show *machiya* characteristic of the Sanneizaka district, in which homes were built along paths up the slope to Kiyomizu temple. Many of these shops have been catering to pilgrims to the famed temple for centuries, serving refreshments and trinkets to the thousands who travel here each year to pray.

The steep cobblestone paths leading up the hill can be difficult to navigate on a rainy day, of which there are many in this part of Kyoto. This has led to the area's popular nickname, Sannenzaka. *Sannen* means "three years" and that is how many years of bad luck, superstition has it, will befall anyone who falls down the slippery steps. Cautious pilgrims are comforted here in the knowledge that misfortune can be avoided with the purchase of a good luck charm in the shape of a gourd at the shop at the bottom of the steepest stone steps along the way. Marketing savvy and superstition appear to work hand in hand at times like these. The protected district begins at the foot of Ninenzaka, the "two-year slope," and you've guessed it, you'd better watch your step here as well.

The Sanneizaka district is one of the best remaining representatives of a *monzencho*. Some of the *machiya* here on the eastern edge of the city are among the oldest in Kyoto, as they were spared much of the frequent fire damage suffered in the heart of the capital below.

Mushiko-mado are characteristic of Kyoto's oldest houses. These slatted second-floor windows seem to be cut out of the clay walls themselves, and legend has it that in feudal times, when commoners were forced to prostrate themselves before passing warlords, these windows permitted ambitious merchants to keep "a head above" their lords, observing them secretly from their hidden vantage point as they passed through the streets below. Other less romantic observers suggest that ventilation was the primary concern, but a stroll up Sanneizaka is no time for analysis. You are here to celebrate the journey with all the other hopeful pilgrims out for the day.

Wooden shutters open the shop fronts of the oldest houses on the path to the street during the daytime, closing at night to afford their keepers some needed privacy. Here, as in many of

Along the paths that lead to Kiyomizu-dera are remnants of the once flourishing Kiyomizu-yaki potteries whose climbing kilns lined the hills in this district until two decades ago, when environmental concerns forced their relocation. Many of the original Kiyomizu-yaki potters still sell their delicate wares in shops along this popular street.

The Kiyomizu district was once the home of one of Japan's most famous ceramic artists, Nonomura Ninsei, who lived in this district in the seventeenth century. The delicate touch of this tea jar is characteristic of Ninsei, whose style influenced such ceramic masters as Ogata Kenzan, one of Ninsei's students. Kenzan's increasingly abstract and boldly decorative style left its mark on much of Japanese art thereafter.

the traditional neighborhoods of Kyoto, many people still live in the tatami-mat rooms behind the shops they work in. The sense of community in districts like this throughout Kyoto reflects the commitment to the neighborhood that comes from people who work and live together in the same place, though it is a way of life that is sadly disappearing.

Yasaka Pagoda, rebuilt in its present form in 1440, is the visual and spiritual landmark that has anchored this neighborhood for hundreds of years. Once the tallest structure in the city, it is the oldest wooden structure standing in Kyoto and all that remains of a temple called Hokan-ji that was destroyed by fire centuries ago. The pagoda is a Buddhist symbol that descended originally from the Indian stupa, mounds in which relics of the Buddha were enshrined. The Japanese version of this symbol is constructed around a gigantic central wooden pole, with interlocking wooden posts and beams, held together without nails, giving it the flexibility to withstand the frequent earthquakes that have long plagued the Japanese archipelago. Yasaka Pagoda sits quietly along the edges of this popular neighborhood, standing watch as it always has, now over the bustle of the twenty- first century.

Pottery was the main trade of the Kiyomizu district. During the sixteenth century, a number of potters built *noborigama*, or climbing kilns, on these slopes, and created the fine hand-painted porcelain ware known today as Kiyomizu-yaki. Because Kyoto was the home of the imperial court

Shops along the slopes of Ninenzaka and Sanneizaka offer delicately painted wares that echo the beauty of Ninsei's masterworks of centuries ago.

GETTING THERE: Yasaka Jinja shrine is a brief walk east down Shijo-dori avenue from downtown Kyoto or a short taxi ride from most major hotels.

SUGGESTED COURSE: **1** Yasaka Jinja shrine → **2** Ishibe-koji → **3** Kodai-ji temple → **4** Ninenzaka → **5** Yasaka Pagoda → **6** Sanneizaka → **7** Kiyomizu-zaka → **8** Kiyomizu-dera temple (World Cultural Heritage Site) → **9** Kawai Kanjiro Memorial House.

ARCHITECTURAL FEATURES: *Mushiko-mado* windows, cut into the clay walls of the low, second stories of the houses in the Sanneizaka *monzencho* district, characterize one of the oldest styles of *machiya* built in Kyoto. Lighter in appearance than the heavily slatted façades of some of the *machiya* in downtown Kyoto, these shops and homes have a more open and hospitable feeling that comes from serving the constant flow of pilgrims to Kiyomizu-dera temple.

BEST TIME OF DAY: Early morning, just as the shops begin to open, is the best time of day to get a sense of this area as a residential neighborhood. Once the throngs of

tourists set in at midday, the shopping is grand, but patience may be required to brave the crowds that flock each day to the tourist mecca on the hill above.

BEST SEASON: Sanneizaka is a pleasure to visit any time of year, but the winter months can be delightful, as this is the season for *yudofu*, the one-pot simmered tofu specialty of the district. Visit Okutan on the curve at the bottom of Sanneizaka, just before it turns down the hill to Ninenzaka. Okutan is an elegant traditional restaurant in a former villa that cannot be seen from the main path. It is a wonderful retreat from the bustling crowds and an excellent place to enjoy a *yudofu* lunch overlooking a lovely garden.

FOR THE TAXI DRIVER:
Yasaka Jinja mae made itte-kudasai.
八坂神社前まで行ってください。
Please take me to the front of Yasaka Jinja shrine.

ESTIMATED TIME: Half a day.

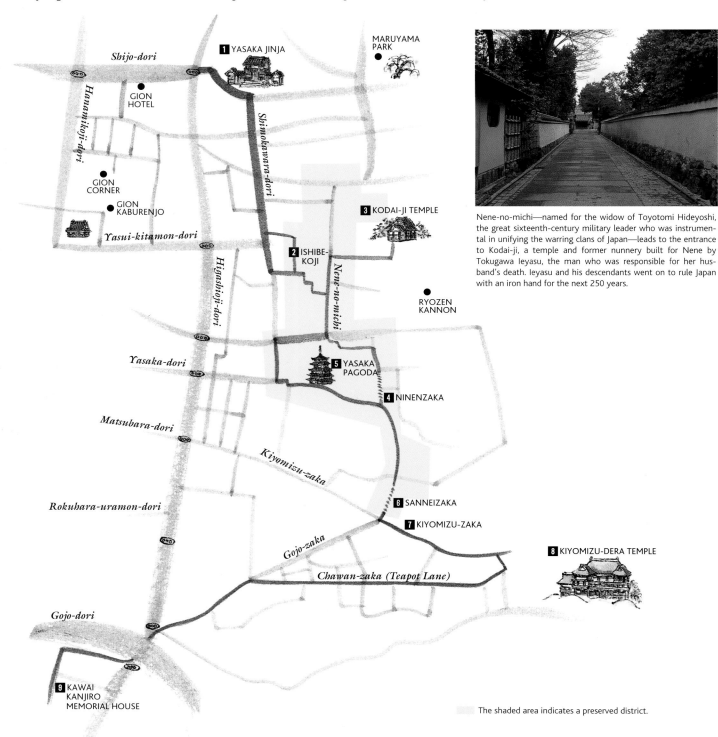

Nene-no-michi—named for the widow of Toyotomi Hideyoshi, the great sixteenth-century military leader who was instrumental in unifying the warring clans of Japan—leads to the entrance to Kodai-ji, a temple and former nunnery built for Nene by Tokugawa Ieyasu, the man who was responsible for her husband's death. Ieyasu and his descendants went on to rule Japan with an iron hand for the next 250 years.

The shaded area indicates a preserved district.

Ishibe-koji, a quiet little alleyway, known for the beauty of the walls that line it, is a lovely walk past private homes, small galleries, cozy restaurants, and a very special little *ryokan* called Uemura. Tell my friend, Mrs. Uemura, that "Dai-an" sent you.

for over ten centuries, the local pottery has a light, decorative flair that reflects the tastes of the old aristocracy and is characterized by delicate painting in blue, red, yellow, and green on a white porcelain background, often accented with gold. The Kiyomizu kilns were moved to Yamashina, west of the Eastern Mountains, due to twentieth-century environmental regulations, but many of the famous potteries keep studios and shops here at the foot of Kiyomizu.

Besides the fragile beauty of Kiyomizu-yaki, this ceramic district is also known as the home of the revival of a more rustic folk style that was on the verge of disappearing by the turn of the nineteenth century. Be sure to pay your respects at the home of the late Kawai Kanjiro, the noted potter-philosopher and cofounder of the *mingei*, or folk-art movement, in the 1930s. When Japan opened its doors to trade with the West in the Meiji period (1868–1912), suddenly all things Western were in vogue and all things traditionally Japanese were put aside as primitive and old-fashioned. Kawai Kanjiro and his friends Yanagi Soetsu, Hamada Shoji, Bernard Leach, and Kuroda Tatsuaki recognized the enduring strength and beauty of functional objects made by anonymous craftspeople in villages throughout Japan. The movement they began sparked enough interest in handmade folk crafts to save many struggling villages in Japan to the present day.

Achieving considerable fame for his bold and original ceramic designs, Kawai remained true to the spirit of the anonymous country craftsmen. Offered the designation of Living National Treasure, Kawai humbly declined. He never signed a pot, though no one could mistake one of his distinctive works for anyone else's.

His home to the southeast of Gojo and Higashioji streets is open to the public. Although the exterior was designed to match the neighborhood style, Kawai designed the interior in the style of a farmhouse of the Hida-Takayama district in Gifu Prefecture. This quiet potter's studio and kiln are full of the spirit of this remarkable man, who believed above all in *tariki*, a Buddhist belief in a power outside oneself that directs the hand and guides the soul.

The home of Kawai Kanjiro is a must for anyone fond of ceramics and of working with one's heart and hands to make beautiful things. His massive climbing kiln, once the center of activity in this potters' neighborhood, sits now in reverent silence behind the house.

The nape of a powdered neck—a subtle expression of Japanese eroticism, an art perfected by the *maiko*, apprentice geisha, of Gion.

GION SHINBASHI

Kani kaku ni
Gion wa koishi
neru toki mo
makura no shita o
mizu no nagaruru

No matter what they say,
I love Gion.
Even in my sleep,
the sound of water flows
beneath my pillow.

—Yoshii Isamu, 1886–1960

GION IS A WORLD OF THE NIGHT.

Behind its latticed doorways and windows is a world that few are privileged to know—a world for men, wealthy men—run by women, the geisha of Gion. Beside the Shirakawa canal that runs like a seam through this district, the stone monument that bears Yoshii Isamu's poem almost became its epitaph. Yoshii, a consumptive and impoverished poet, lived and died in Gion, cared for by the geisha who gave shelter to their favorite poet in his final years. In his memory, the women of Gion refused to permit their exotic neighborhood to die, petitioning the government to recognize and preserve this entertainment quarter as a historic district in the late 1970s.

Nightfall at the *o-chaya*, the "teahouses" where the geisha entertain their guests.

In its heyday, there were hundreds of geisha living and working in this district. Today only about fifty remain, but as professional entertainers they are among the strongest advocates for maintaining the customs and traditions of Kyoto. A special form of Kyoto dialect, lilting and evasive, is spoken in Gion, almost religiously, and almost nowhere else as pervasively. Shamisen (a three-stringed musical instrument) lessons are attended every morning, and traditional dance is kept alive here through the annual Miyako Odori dance recital. Other traditional entertainment districts exist in Kyoto and elsewhere, but Gion was the height of sophistication among all the geisha quarters in Japan.

The men who visit Gion are still catered to—unbelievably pampered, in fact—here behind the *sudare* reed screens that hide this private world of luxury from public view. Until the decline of the kimono industry, the most frequent visitors were the wealthy kimono merchants of Nishijin. The privileged few still play out their private fantasies here in an elegant atmosphere in which the nuance of meaning in a glance, or a glimpse of the nape of the neck, is more seductive in the Japanese erotic sensibility than any more obvious display of love or lust.

Gion will always be very much a mystery and should remain so. It is the home of an unparalleled tradition and is a neighborhood of the night with all the seductive ambiguity that suggests, "Do they or don't they?" In some cultures, some things are better left unsaid.

From Gion came stunning images of matchless beauties depicted in eighteenth-century *ukiyo-e* woodblock prints. *Ukiyo* was first a Buddhist word that refers to the transitory nature of this world of ours. In the world of the geisha, it refers to that "floating world" in which languid, sad-eyed women draped in hand-painted kimono mourned the coming of dawn—and the inevitable loss of love this life of passion so often held in store. What goes on behind the *bengara-goshi*, the rust-colored latticed windows of Gion? No one can (or will) say for sure. Mystery, after all, is the key to its seductive charm.

Shinbashi is the name of a small bridge built in the early eighteenth century over the Shirakawa river in the northern part of Gion. The triangular block of *o-chaya*, or teahouses, beside

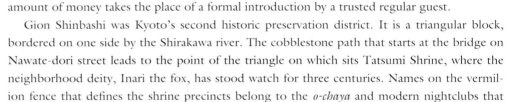

Sudare reed screens, characteristic of this district, conceal from public view the exclusive "floating world" of entertainment in the teahouses along the Shirakawa canal, in the heart of Gion.

it shares its name. *O-chaya* are the places to which geisha (or *geiko*, as they are known in Kyoto) are called to entertain guests. No stranger gains admittance to an *o-chaya* in Gion; no amount of money takes the place of a formal introduction by a trusted regular guest.

Gion Shinbashi was Kyoto's second historic preservation district. It is a triangular block, bordered on one side by the Shirakawa river. The cobblestone path that starts at the bridge on Nawate-dori street leads to the point of the triangle on which sits Tatsumi Shrine, where the neighborhood deity, Inari the fox, has stood watch for three centuries. Names on the vermilion fence that defines the shrine precincts belong to the *o-chaya* and modern nightclubs that make up this district.

Maiko are apprentice geisha, the painted dolls you may see clip-clopping on high platform *pokkori geta*, with their elaborate brocade sashes trailing behind them, if you stroll through Shinbashi just after sunset. Eighteen, nineteen, twenty years old, the *maiko* are the icing on the evening's cake in Gion. While the *geiko* she accompanies carry on the playful conversation (sprinkled with wit and double-entendre), the *maiko* pose and play their pouty parlor games, pouring the saké and pealing the grapes for *danna*, the "lord and master" of the evening, the honored guest who might one day become her own special benefactor.

The geisha of Gion are not viewed as prostitutes, particularly not in modern times. The mere mention of such a notion is guaranteed to arouse an indignant response. They are professional dancers, performers, entertainers, as the character (芸) *gei* implies. As such, they are responsible to this day for keeping many of the traditional performing arts alive in Japan. *Nihon buyo* is a dance form that was derived from kabuki and first developed as an art form by the geisha of Gion. That is one reason why Gion Shinbashi is unique as a historic preservation area. Here, history lives on, as long as the geisha and their special form of entertainment continue. Their world supports an entire population of artisans and craftspeople who make the special wooden shoes, the elaborate hair combs, the colorful dance fans, the oiled paper parasols,

Three *maiko* on their way to entertain guests at a teahouse.

GETTING THERE: Gion Shinbashi is a short walk from the downtown area. Stroll east up Shijo-dori and cross the river. From Sanjo Station, walk south on Nawate-dori past the many antique shops and restaurants, until you come to the Shirakawa canal (**2**). Turn left and you are in the Shinbashi district.

SUGGESTED COURSE: **1** Nawate-dori and Antique Street → **2** Shirakawa canal → **3** "*Kani kaku ni*" stone → **4** Shinbashi bridge → **5** *O-chaya*, or teahouses → **6** Minamiza Kabuki Theater → **7** Kagizen confectionery → **8** Ichiriki *o-chaya* → **9** Gion Corner (evening shows featuring demonstrations of Japanese arts) → **10** Kennin-ji temple → **11** Shinmonzen Antique Street → **12** Pontocho (another of Kyoto's geisha entertainment quarters, lined with restaurants and teahouses; a pleasant evening stroll across the river from Gion).

ARCHITECTURAL FEATURES: The *sudare* reed blinds that hang from all the second-floor windows of the *o-chaya* in Gion are so much a part of the visual character of the district that they are considered a distinguishing architectural feature. They afford privacy for the elite customers who attend regular private banquets at the *o-chaya*.

BEST TIME OF DAY: See Gion in the late afternoon, just as the sun begins to go down. At this time of day, it is not unusual to catch a glimpse of *geiko* and *maiko* as they promenade in all their finery along the side streets from their *okiya*, where they live, to the *o-chaya*, where they are called to entertain. Daytime hours are best for the shops.

BEST TIME OF YEAR: Summertime, when the second-floor windows are thrown open and from behind the *sudare* blinds you can hear the sound of shamisen and the haunting voices of *geiko* singing *nagauta*, the melancholy songs of love in this floating world.

FOR THE TAXI DRIVER:
Nawate-dori no Shirakawa-bashi made itte-kudasai.
縄手通りの白川橋まで行ってください。
Please take me to the Shirakawa Bridge on Nawate-dori street.

ESTIMATED TIME: One hour (not including a performance at Gion Corner).

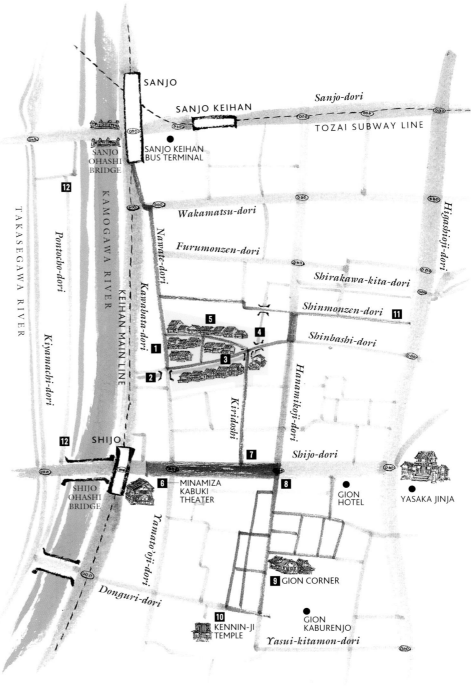

The shaded area indicates a preserved district.

The "*Kani kaku ni*" stone commemorates the beloved poet Yoshii Isamu, who spent his dying days here in the care of the geisha of Gion. The poem inscribed on the stone opens this chapter.

The two-storied teahouses of Gion Shinbashi share walls (and no doubt secrets) with their neighbors on either side.

the musical instruments, and all the other special accoutrements of their trade. Some of Kyoto's finest *ryotei*, as the high-class traditional restaurants are known, can be found tucked away on the back streets of Gion. It is doubtful whether the best of formal *Kyo-ryori kaiseki* cuisine would survive if the world of the geisha were not kept alive. But the geisha do survive, spending years of their lives in rigorous training at tea ceremony, learning traditional flower arrangement, practicing the shamisen, as well learning to master the subtle art of traditional dance.

In the south part of Gion, on the southeast corner of Shijo-dori at Hanamikoji, stands the legendary Ichiriki, the three-hundred-year-old *o-chaya*. It was here in the seventeenth century that Oishi Yoshio, the leader of the famous forty-seven *ronin*, pretended to lose himself in a life of debauchery while secretly plotting his revenge against the corrupt shogunal official responsible for his master's unjust death. The dusky red color of the walls of Ichiriki, once characteristic of the whole Gion district, are now scarcely found anywhere else.

The Minamiza Kabuki Theater, beside the Kamogawa river on Shijo-dori avenue, dates to the early seventeenth century and is the oldest theater in Japan. The southern of two original theaters that faced each other across Shijo-dori, the present Minamiza building was constructed in 1929 and fully restored in recent years. It evokes the original spirit of kabuki, and is crowded with passionate devotees every December, when the Kaomise (Face Showing) Festival is held. Major stars from Tokyo and all over Japan "put in an appearance" on stage at the Minamiza during this month-long event.

Minamiza, Kyoto's kabuki theater, hosts the annual Kaomise kabuki performances at which everyone who is anyone in Kyoto society "shows their face" each year in December. The vertical wooden plaques above the entrance list the participants for 2001.

Kabuki began in Kyoto in the seventeenth century, when a young woman known as Izumo-no-Okuni danced on the banks of the Kamogawa before a crowd of enthusiastic fans. It was not until the shogun banned women from the stage for "corrupting public morals" that female impersonators took over their role in kabuki. The first "geisha" were male performers who danced and entertained in the teahouses in the district that surrounded the kabuki theaters.

At the heart of this gloriously decadent world you will find something quite unexpected, Kyoto's oldest, and one of its largest Zen Buddhist temples, Kennin-ji. During the Edo period (1600–1868), the common people were forbidden to travel outside their own districts, except for the purpose of a religious pilgrimage, which naturally became the accepted excuse for an excursion to the ancient capital. Stroll through the grounds of Kennin-ji for a quiet moment and observe where many a retired geisha spends her final years.

The brilliance of elaborate *obi* sashes, woven with gold threads and adorned with jeweled *obidome* broaches, marks the costume of the young *maiko* apprentices.

◀ Ichiriki, one of the most famous *o-chaya* teahouses in Japan, is among the most elegant in the city—a rich combination of textures and patterns, with its rust-colored walls, finely slatted windows, bamboo *inuyarai* coverings, and meticulously tiled roofs.

嵯峨野　鳥居本

SAGANO TORIIMOTO

In the suburbs of Kyoto, a form of roof and ridge may often be seen. In this form the supplementary roof is more sharply defined; the corners of it are slightly turned up as in the temple roof. To be more definite, the main roof, which is a hipped roof, has built upon it a low upper-roof, which is a gable; and upon this rests, like a separate structure, a continuous saddle of thatch, having upon its back a few bamboos running longitudinally, and across the whole a number of narrow saddles of thatch sheathed with bark, and over all a long bamboo bound to the ridge with cords. These roofs, broad and thick-eaved, with their deep-set, heavily latticed smoke windows, and the warm brown thatch, form a pleasing contrast to the thin-shingled roofs of the poorer neighboring houses.

—Edward S. Morse, 1887

Candles are lit annually in memory of scores of unknown souls whose final resting place is marked by individually carved stone markers here at Adashino Nenbutsu-ji temple, and above it on the hillside at Otagi Nenbutsu-ji (inset).

The legendary bamboo forests of Sagano Toriimoto district echo the legends of love and exile that haunt this former refuge of emperors and their concubines. ▶

THE "POORER NEIGHBORING HOUSES" Morse referred to

over a hundred years ago no longer exist in Sagano. Fortunately, however, a few of the magnificent thatched country homes he so admired do remain and are preserved in the Sagano district by law.

Around the turn of the nineteenth century, most homes in the Japanese countryside had thatched roofs. Today there are not very many left. For one thing, they are considered fire

Playfully hand-painted Saga folk masks are a traditional souvenir of this once rural district. These masks are the work of master craftsman Fujiwara Fuseki.

hazards; for another, there is almost no one left who knows how to repair them. The special type of reed used (*yoshi*) is becoming harder and harder to obtain as the wetlands disappear, and the days when an entire community gathered to help rebuild one farmer's rooftop are all but forgotten. The handful of thatched rooftops that remain on the old road that leads up to the bright vermilion gateway (*torii*) of Atago Shrine are a symbol of rural Japan—the way it was.

Atago Shrine is a steep two-hour hike straight up the side of Mt. Atago in the western part of Kyoto. The God Who Prevents Fires lives there, and for several centuries, the citizens of Kyoto have trudged dutifully up the steps to keep their city safe from the flames that destroyed it time and again in the past.

At one time, the entire city of Kyoto was built only of wood, thatch, and tiles, and people lived with the constant threat of fire. Because the rowhouses of Kyoto share wooden walls with their neighbors on both sides, my fire is your fire, so once a month, everyone marched up Mt. Atago to pray.

The Tenmei Fire of 1788 ranks as one of the biggest fires in the history of the world; only the fire that followed the Great Tokyo Earthquake in 1923 rivals it in Japanese history. It started in a money-changer's shop in the southwestern part of the city at 9 A.M. By the next morning, eighty percent of the city, everything west of the Kamogawa river, lay in ashes. The red plastic fire

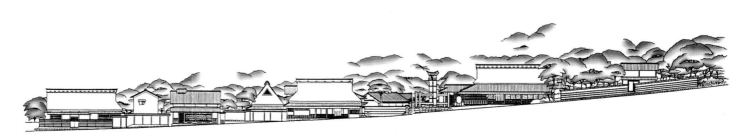

The expansive thatched rooftops once found all around the outskirts of Kyoto now remain only here along this last sloping path up to Mt. Atago.

SAGANO TORIIMOTO 嵯峨野 鳥居本

GETTING THERE: Accessible by bus or train. By bus, take City Bus No. 11 from Sanjo Keihan Bus Terminal (see the map of Gion on page 23). Get off at Arashiyama. By train, take the Keifuku Arashiyama Line from Shijo-Omiya Station and get off at Arashiyama. From here you can walk down a block or two to the Togetsu-kyo Bridge (**10**) to get your bearings. This is a large area to cover in one day on foot. An alternative is to rent a bicycle near the bridge or near Arashiyama Station. Or consider taking a taxi from the bridge to Toriimoto. If you start your walk up at Toriimoto (**1**), you can work your way slowly back down to Arashiyama and the river.

SUGGESTED COURSE: **1** Toriimoto (thatched-roof houses) → **2** Adashino Nenbutsu-ji → **3** Gio-ji → **4** Nison-in → **5** Rakushi-sha → **6** Okochi Sanso Villa → **7** Bamboo path → **8** Nonomiya Shrine → **9** Tenryu-ji temple → **10** Togetsu-kyo Bridge.

FOR THE TAXI DRIVER:
Arashiyama no Togetsu-kyo made itte-kudasai.
嵐山の渡月橋まで行ってください。
Please take me to the Togetsu-kyo Bridge in Arashiyama.

ESTIMATED TIME: One full day.

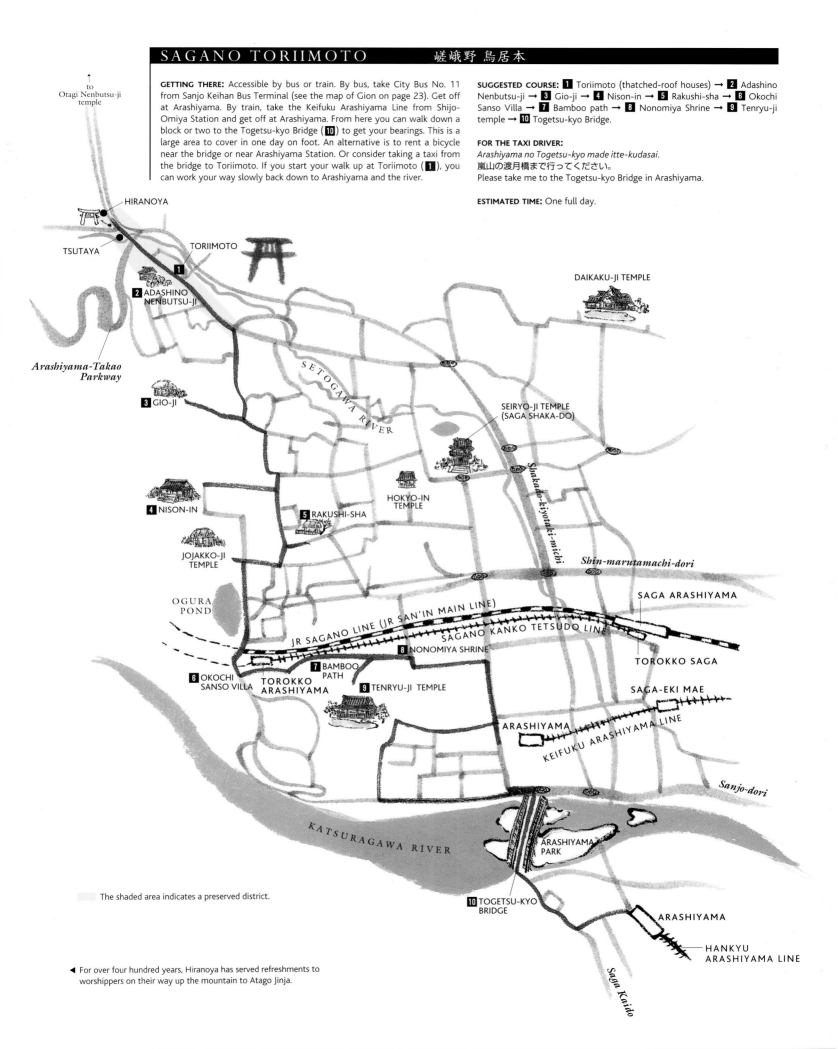

The shaded area indicates a preserved district.

◄ For over four hundred years, Hiranoya has served refreshments to worshippers on their way up the mountain to Atago Jinja.

The majestic thatched-roof homes of Toriimoto.

buckets you see beside the doorway of many of the old houses in Kyoto today are a reminder of the danger of fire.

The road down from Toriimoto leads past Adashino Nenbutsu-ji, with hundreds of stone buddhas that mark the graves of nameless men and women who died penniless or were simply forgotten centuries ago—Kyoto's "boot hill." There are many small temples along the way, like Gio-ji, where a famed beauty, the banished mistress of a shogun, lived out her life in the nunnery; a poet's hut, Rakushi-sha, where haiku poet Basho himself spent time with a friend during his travels; the exquisite and eccentric Okochi Sanso, a villa owned by a silent-movie star who spent the last thirty years of his life land-scaping the entire mountainside. Walk through Tenryu-ji temple and its magnificent gardens to the river or detour down the bamboo-lined path to Nonomiya Shrine, famous for jilted lovers and a sad scene from *The Tale of Genji*. Go all the way down to Arashiyama beside the Oigawa river, where the Togetsu-kyo Bridge marks the favorite former playground of emperors and warlords. Far removed from palace life in Kyoto, the Sagano district, with its lush bamboo forests, steep-walled ravines, quiet rice fields and legends of romance, has always been famous as a place of escape.

Nison-in, the Temple of Two Venerables, is dedicated to two manifestations of the Buddha—Shakyamuni, the historical Buddha who helps us through the difficulties of this world, and Amida, the Buddha of the Pure Land, who guides us toward the world hereafter. The main gate of Nison-in was once a part of ruler Toyotomi Hideyoshi's grand palace in Fushimi.

Basho, humbled by the beauty of this simple setting and no doubt reminded, as anyone is who visits today, that one cannot measure wealth in gold, wrote many of his finest poems in this little country hut, known as Rakushi-sha.

Handmade straw *takarabune* ("treasure boats") are characteristic decorations in Kamigamo Shaké-machi that adorn homes and farmhouses while assuring good luck in the new year.

The abstract beauty of the "Twin Peaks of Heaven" sand sculpture in the courtyard of Kamigamo Jinja channel the favor of the gods enshrined in one of Kyoto's oldest Shinto shrines. ▶

KAMIGAMO SHAKÉ-MACHI

The twilight dim, the gentle breeze
By Nara-no-Ogawa Stream
The splash of worshipers who wash
Before the shrine, all seem
A perfect summer's dream.
—Fujiwara Iyetaka, from *Hyakunin Isshu*, 1237

GODDESS TAMAYORI-HIME led a very exciting life. While bathing in a stream one day in northern Kyoto, she noticed a bright red arrow floating in the water and couldn't resist taking it home. For good luck, she tucked it under her pillow, only to be awakened at midnight to find that the arrow had turned into a dashing young man, "and the goddess was subsequently with child," as legend discreetly puts it. This was only the first of many surprises in store for Her Heavenly Highness. She soon gave birth to Wakeikazuchi, who burst from her womb, exploding through the rooftop and into the night sky as the God of Thunder and Rain, who dwells to this day in all his celestial impetuousness at Kamigamo Shrine.

Kamigamo Jinja was originally the personal shrine of the Kamo family, who inhabited this valley for centuries before Emperor Kanmu built his capital here in 794. By the time Kanmu arrived, the God of Thunder had already earned himself quite a reputation for his violent temper, the apparent cause of continual floods and storms that plagued the area. Emperor Kanmu instructed his emissaries to pay their respects at Kamigamo Shrine in a formal procession to ensure the God of Thunder was appeased.

◄ The Romon Gate of Kamigamo Shrine leads to the inner shrine where the God of Thunder was enshrined long before the city of Kyoto was founded in 794.

The sacred Nara-no-ogawa flows along the canals that connect the *shaké-machi* homes of the priests who tended Kamigamo Shrine for centuries. The clay walls of these old estates have openings through which water from the sacred stream enters the gardens, where in centuries past the priests performed daily ceremonial ritual bathing ceremonies to purify themselves before going up to the grand shrine.

Long, low clay walls characterize the Kamigamo Shaké-machi district, once the home of priest attendants of Kamigamo shrine.

Aoi Matsuri, one of Kyoto's three most important festivals, is held each year on May 15, when an imperial messenger proceeds from the former palace to the shrine in an elaborate procession of ox-drawn carts to pray for peace and an abundant harvest. Until the thirteenth century, a virgin princess from the imperial family was always in attendance at Kamigamo, where the lusty legend of the Thunder God's birth won him a subsequent role as the God of Fertility. The carefully tended pair of sand cones that stand in the shrine precincts represents the mountains through which Wakeikazuchi communicates with this mortal plane. Kamigamo Shrine is also a popular place for local people, who can be seen almost any day of the week having their weddings and newborn babies blessed by priests inside the shrine's special ceremonial hall.

Dating to the seventh century, Kamigamo Jinja is one of the oldest and most revered shrines in Kyoto, and the priests whose families have attended it for centuries dwelt in the neighborhood that surrounds it—the *shaké-machi* of Kamigamo. The Nara-no-ogawa stream that runs through the grounds of the shrine is sacred, and for centuries shrine priests have built their homes along its banks just outside the precincts of the shrine.

The sacred stream enters a canal and, if you follow narrow Kusunoki-dori (which takes its

The old tiered dams along the nearby Kamogawa river now stand empty, where once they were lined with wooden barrels during pickling season. The district was famous for an abundance of fresh local produce and delicious *senmaizuke* pickles, which can still be found in traditional *tsukemono* pickle shops in the area.

name from the giant *kusunoki*, or camphor tree, around which it winds) running east along the canal, you pass the clay-walled *shaké-machi* homes, one of which, the Nishimura House, is a historic landmark open to the public daily (except in winter). A winding stream flows through the classic Heian-style gardens of this and other *shaké-machi* homes, drawing upon the sacred water let in from the canal. The resident priests once bathed in small, deep pools of water in their gardens as part of a purification rite before proceeding to the shrine for official ceremonies. There were once over 275 *shaké-machi* households in the Kamigamo district. By the seventeenth century they had formed a tightly knit township around the shrine and were both under Kamigamo's spiritual protection and responsible for defending it in times of trouble. A system of moats encircled the town outside the shrine precincts during the feudal ages to help defend it from fires and wars, as well as for irrigation.

Architecturally, the *shaké-machi* homes are open and spacious in this once rural district, compared with the city dwellings in the middle of Kyoto, where land is at such a premium. The thick clay walls surrounding each compound are characteristic of *shaké-machi* homes. Here, on the outer edges of the city at the foot of the Kitayama hills, one can still find traditional farmhouses, with compact rice paddies and meticulously tended vegetable gardens.

The district is famous for its special produce, particularly for *Kamo-nasu*, a special round variety of eggplant that is a popular summer treat in Kyoto. It is not unusual to see women from the Kamigamo district pulling heavy carts of homegrown vegetables through the streets to sell to individual households in midtown.

Pickles, or *tsukemono*, a necessary condiment served with Japanese rice, are another Kamigamo specialty. Along Kusunoki-dori you'll find Narita, one of Kyoto's finest pickle shops in a restored *shaké-machi* home. Note the high ceiling with its rough-hewn post-and-beam construction, held together by an elaborate joinery system without the use of nails.

Make your way further east to the tiny neighborhood shrine, Ota Jinja, where people come to pray for good health, luck in marriage, and even for success on the stage. The pond beside it is filled with lovely *kakitsubata* iris, which bloom twice, in May and early June, attracting scores of avid photographers and sightseers.

Beyond the pond is the entrance gate to Azekura, a three-hundred-year-old saké warehouse that was moved to this site all the way from Nara over thirty years ago by a wealthy Kyoto ki-

Japanese pickles made from *suguki*, a particularly delectable root vegetable related to the turnip, are a local specialty.

mono merchant. The huge wooden structure, with its exposed beams and high ceilings, now holds a modern restaurant. Upstairs is an exhibition and performance space, used occasionally for kimono exhibits and local dance and drama performances. The garden surrounding Azekura offers an opportunity for a stroll through a bamboo grove to a teahouse cantilevered on the side of the hill.

Time and water are two of the elements that make the Kamigamo district special among the old neighborhoods of Kyoto. Older than the city of Kyoto itself, this neighborhood has retained much of its quiet rural atmosphere, managing to stay somehow on the fringe. The waters of Nara-no-ogawa stream that flow through the *shaké-machi* here recall the traditional Japanese reverence for water as a source of purification for both body and soul.

Women preparing *suguki* for *tsukemono* pickles, a necessary part of the traditional Japanese meal.

KAMIGAMO SHAKÉ-MACHI　上賀茂　社家町

GETTING THERE: Take City Bus No. 4 or 37 from Sanjo Keihan Bus Terminal (see the map of Gion on page 23) and get off at Kamigamo Jinja-mae. Return by walking further east, past Azekura to Midorogaike Pond, catching the No. 4 bus. By train, take the Karasuma Subway Line to Kitayama Station. Ota Shrine (**5**) is about one kilometer from the station.

SUGGESTED COURSE: **1** Kamigamo Jinja (World Cultural Heritage Site) → **2** *Shaké-machi* houses → **3** Narita pickle shop → **4** Nishimura House → **5** Ota Shrine → **6** Azekura.

ARCHITECTURAL FEATURES: The clay-walled *shaké-machi* houses along Kusunoki-dori and the Heian-style gardens with their winding streams are the most distinctive features of this district, along with the remaining farmhouses with their high-beamed ceilings.

BEST TIME OF DAY: Late morning when the local shops open or early on a summer evening when the light is lovely and the day's heat has subsided.

BEST SEASON: Visit in May around Aoi Matsuri (May 15) to see the festival and iris pond beside Ota Shrine. Late fall or early winter is the time when much of the pickling is done, a quieter time for a peaceful stroll.

FOR THE TAXI DRIVER:
Kamigamo Jinja mae made itte-kudasai.
上賀茂神社前まで行ってください。
Please take me to the front of Kamigamo Shrine.

ESTIMATED TIME: Three hours.

The sea of delicate purple iris, for which the pond at the tiny Ota Shrine is famous, bloom in May and early June.

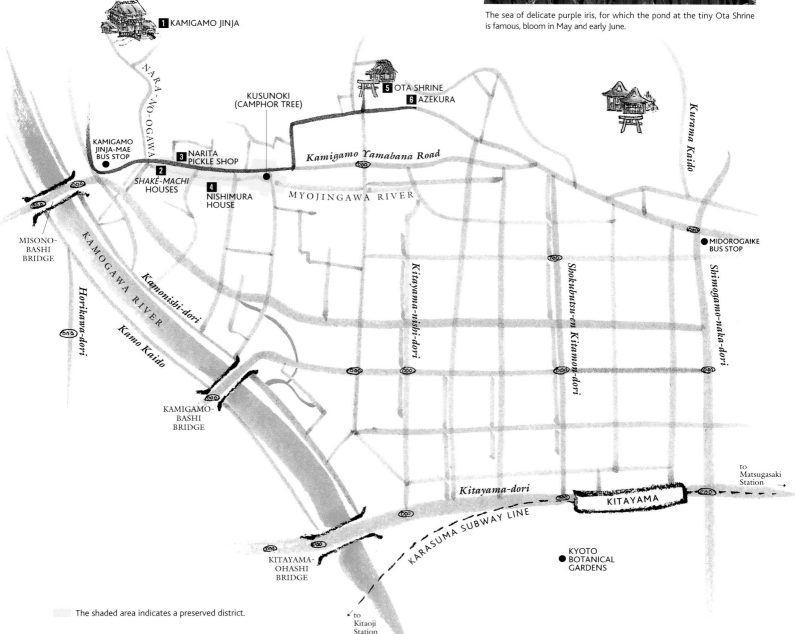

The shaded area indicates a preserved district.

Only a few handlooms remain in Nishijin that produce the unmatched beauty of *tsuzure-ori* kimono sashes.

N I S H I J I N

I bring no prayers on colored silk
to deck thy shrine today,
but take instead these maple leaves
that grow at Mt. Tamuke—
finer than silk are they.
    Sugawara-no-Michizane, from *Hyakunin no Isshu*

KATTAN, KOTTON... KATTAN, *kotton ... kattan, kotton ...* the rattle of twenty thousand weavers' looms beats out a pattern that is centuries old—the street music of Nishijin. The word for "loom" in Japanese is *hata*, perhaps because these weavers were descendants of the Hata family, Korean immigrants who brought their craft to Kyoto before the imperial court moved to this valley in 794.

The Nishijin district in the northwestern corner of Kyoto, though its boundaries are not clearly defined, stretches roughly east and west between Horikawa and Nishi-oji, and north and south between Kita-oji and Nakadachiuri-dori. For over four and a half centuries, Nishijin was the home of the craftsmen and women who produced the exquisite silk brocade Nishijin-ori textiles, which are among the finest in the world.

Though much of the fabric produced here since the turn of the century has been done on Western-style Jacquard looms (most of which are now automated), there are still a few traditional *te-bata* hand looms left in Nishijin today. One of the most complicated and time-

consuming types of traditional weaving done in Nishijin is known as *tsuzure-ori*, a process in which the weaver files grooves in her fingernails to separate the weave and tighten the weft enough to achieve the intricate pictorial quality for which this fabric is known.

In accordance with tradition, no one person produces cloth from start to finish by herself. Dozens of separate craftspeople are contracted to complete each of the many steps of the weaving process. One household dyes the thread, another threads the looms, one weaves, another stretches. There are even people in Nishijin who specialize only in steaming newly completed fabrics—or simply in carrying works in process from one household to the next.

Finally, the *obi* sashes and kimono of Nishijin are sold under the name of one of the famous merchants in the district who contracts individual craftspeople and their workshops. A chain of "middlemen" has long stood between the weaver and buyer, a system that evolved into the complicated distribution system for which Japanese business is still known today. World-famous names like Daimaru, Takashimaya, and Mitsui were all originally kimono merchants from Kyoto.

The once-thriving district may have survived the long history of natural and manmade disasters that have destroyed Kyoto repeatedly over the centuries, but with fewer Japanese wearing kimono today, the kimono industry has rapidly declined, and with it the old *machiya* that housed the weavers of Nishijin are disappearing every day.

Until recently, Nishijin was considered a still viable industrial area and was not officially recognized as a preservation district. With the economic changes taking place in these neighborhoods, a new ordinance was passed recently that places some restrictions on development in parts of Nishijin. Unfortunately, this has come too late for much of the traditional urban landscape to survive. However, some local residents have begun the costly task of restoring and preserving their Nishijin *machiya* privately, as has Kazuhiko Mizuno, whose beautiful photography graces these pages. His home and photo gallery in Nishijin offer a chance for visitors to step inside a traditional *machiya* for a glimpse of what life once was like in Nishijin.

Children at play in one of the narrow back streets of Nishijin, the alleys of traditional neighborhoods far too narrow for cars to invade.

His Machiya Photo Museum is open to the public by appointment only. (Send a fax in English or Japanese to 075–431–5511. Admission is free.) The Aizen Kobo house and its indigo-dying workshop is another such hidden treasure.

For the time being, behind just a few of the remaining tightly slatted *senbon-goshi*, or thousand-fingered latticed windows, the production of elaborate gold brocade and silk damask goes on anonymously in the workshops of a handful of weavers and loom threaders of Nishijin. A rare glimpse through one of these latticed windows at dyers hanging their colorful threads from poles between the rafters in the back rooms may be all you'll get. Or follow the clack and rattle of the looms to an open doorway in summer, and you may get a peak down the breezeway at one of the Nishijin weavers working at a traditional loom. Hold that vision—it may not be there to appreciate for long.

◀ Detail from a costume of the noh theater, woven in *karaori* style, a remarkable Japanese weaving technique invented to replicate the hand-embroidered patterns of Chinese imperial robes.

Brilliantly dyed silk threads line the walls of Textile Tatsumi, an *obi* maker's workshop. Each finished woven sash from Nishijin is the work of countless independent craftspeople—dyers, loom threaders, weavers, steamers, and others—who work together to create a finished piece. ▶

Few of the famed *obi* houses, like the landmark Obiya Sute-matsu, remain in business today, as the kimono has become relegated to ceremonial occasions. The dark, heavily gridded façades of textile houses in the old garment district have their own timeless beauty.

The Jacquard loom was brought from France to Kyoto in the nineteenth century, causing a surge in the textile business, whose looms had no automated parts until then.

This treasured eighteenth-century noh robe, with the Autumn Grasses pattern in the *karaori* style, was woven on the looms of Nishijin.

Once an ocean of tile roofs, Kyoto now supports only a few isolated views such as this one. Modern buildings rise every day in this once traditional neighborhood of weavers, though preservationists are working hard to save some of the last remaining areas.

KITANO TENMANGU AND KAMISHICHIKEN

The Nishijin district is divided roughly in half by Senbon-dori, a long avenue of individual shops and markets that is the center of life here. Further west lies Kitano Tenmangu shrine, about a block east of Nishi-oji on Imadegawa-dori. It was established in the tenth century and is dedicated to Sugawara-no-Michizane, a poet, scholar, and imperial minister who died in exile after challenging the powerful Fujiwara family. It is said that shortly after his death in 903 the restless spirit of Michizane appeared to a woman in a dream, promising that if he were enshrined at Kitano, he would stop the devastating series of plagues, fires, and floods that was afflicting the capital, reportedly a result of Michizane's vengeance.

The scholarly Sugawara-no-Michizane is worshipped today as Tenjin-sama, the God of Calligraphy, and is considered the patron saint of all students. They flock here each year to pray for success in Japan's rigorously competitive school entrance exams, writing their prayers on wooden *ema* tablets to hang before Kitano Tenjin, whose special ceremony is still observed here on the twenty-fifth of every month.

Such shrine festivals have attracted itinerant merchants to shrine grounds for centuries. In the past both shrines and temples served as "free-trade zones" where merchants could come to sell their wares, protected within the sacred precincts from robbers and thieves. The shrine at Kitano is one of two such places where this custom continues, the other being Toji temple, south of Kyoto Station, which holds its market on the twenty-first and an antique market on the first Sunday of every month.

On the twenty-fifth of each month, an enormous flea market and people's fair is held all day in and around the shrine grounds, with merchants selling everything from antique kimono and

Kitano Tenmangu shrine lies in the western quarter of the Nishijin district, where it was built in the tenth century in memory of a court nobleman named Sugawara-no-Michizane, the patron saint of poets and scholars.

ceramics to ground chili pepper and hot bean cakes. Farmers from outlying districts bring vegetables and plants for sale. There is something for everyone, and everyone seems to come along, as they have for centuries.

Traditional entertainment quarters are another secular phenomenon that came into being outside the gates of many of Kyoto's most revered temples and shrines. During the totalitarian reign of the Tokugawa shogunate (1603–1868), commoners were forbidden to travel outside their districts—unless it was to make a "spiritual pilgrimage" to a famous religious site. Hence, the "pilgrimage" became a marvelous excuse to travel to faraway Kyoto and sample the many (and universal) temptations of big city life along the way. Teahouses or *o-chaya*, serving thirsty travelers, lined the roads to major religious sites, and the term became a euphemism for establishments where the geisha entertained.

Just a block east of the shrine is a neighborhood known as Kamishichiken, a geisha quarter that is older than its more famous cousin, Gion. The name refers to the first "seven houses" in the neighborhood, said to have been originally constructed of wood left over from repairs to Kitano Tenmangu shrine in the Muromachi period (1333–1568). Once a year, there is a dance festival here during which the geisha of Kamishichiken perform for the public, an occasion not to miss. Since the triangular block of *o-chaya* here is less frequented today than other entertainment quarters in the downtown area, it makes a quiet place to stroll. In February, the *maiko* apprentice geisha of Kamishichiken serve tea in an elegant ceremony at Kitano Tenmangu.

THE TEA CEREMONY

Kitano Tenmangu shrine was the scene of one of the most extravagant tea ceremonies in Japanese history, held by the great sixteenth-century military leader Toyotomi Hideyoshi. A re-enactment of that event, called Kencha-sai, is held here every year on December 1. Hideyoshi was a humble foot soldier who rose through the ranks to become one of Japan's most important military leaders. His taste for extravagant displays of the power and wealth he achieved was shunned by tea master Sen-no-Rikyu, whose *wabi* style of a simple tea reflected the Buddhist-influences of appreciating the refined elegance of the unadorned.

Three of the great schools of *chanoyu*, or tea ceremony—Urasenke, Omotesenke, Mushanokoji-senke—were founded by descendants of Sen-no-Rikyu, and are located on the southeastern edge of Nishijin. The last two are not open to the public, but Urasenke has a modern center, with a museum, a school, and regular demonstrations.

The black Raku teabowl known as "Amadera" by the master potter Chojiro, one of Sen-no-Rikyu's favorite craftsmen.

Not far from here is the home and workshop of the Raku family of ceramic artists, whose ancestor was one of the ten master craftsmen appointed by Sen-no-Rikyu in the sixteenth century to make objects for *chanoyu*. The current descendant is Raku Kichizaemon, whose elegant and innovative tea bowls are on display here with those of previous generations in the family museum next door to the family home. Among Western artists, the word *raku* has come to refer to a low-fired, glazed ceramic technique that produces a rough, often iridescent, effect. The Raku Museum is a gem that is not to be missed by anyone who wishes to experience the understated elegance of the original raku ware.

NISHIJIN 西陣

GETTING THERE: Take City Bus No. 8, 10, or 51 and get off at Kitano Tenmangu (**1**).

SUGGESTED COURSE: **1** Kitano Tenmangu shrine (if you visit the flea market on the twenty-fifth of the month, get there early in the morning) → **2** Kamishichiken teahouses → **3** Senbon Shaka-do → **4** Urasenke → **5** Nishijin Textile Center (housed in a modern building, it is part museum, part gift shop, and part exhibition center, featuring kimono fashion shows and weaving demonstrations). → **6** Raku Museum.

ARCHITECTURAL FEATURES: The *senbon goshi*, or thousand-fingered latticed windows, and white-washed clay walls of the weaving district are two of its most striking characteristics. Look for the heavy *noren* curtains that bear the family crests of the major *obi* sash houses throughout Nishijin.

BEST TIME OF DAY: Early morning on the twenty-fifth day of every month is a good time to start your walk with a visit to the flea market (unless you purchase something you have to carry with you!). Walking from one end of Nishijin to the other can take most of the day.

BEST SEASON: Early spring when the plum blossoms bloom at Kitano Tenmangu shrine is a good time to go, or the twenty-fifth of every month, when the flea market takes place there.

FOR THE TAXI DRIVER:
Kitano Tenmangu mae made itte-kudasai.
北野天満宮前まで行ってください。
Please take me to the front of Kitano Tenmangu shrine.

ESTIMATED TIME: Half a day.

A popular flea market takes place on the hallowed grounds of Kitano Tenmangu shrine on the twenty-fifth of every month, part of a festival day that honors the memory of Sugawara-no-Michizane and brings the neighborhood together.

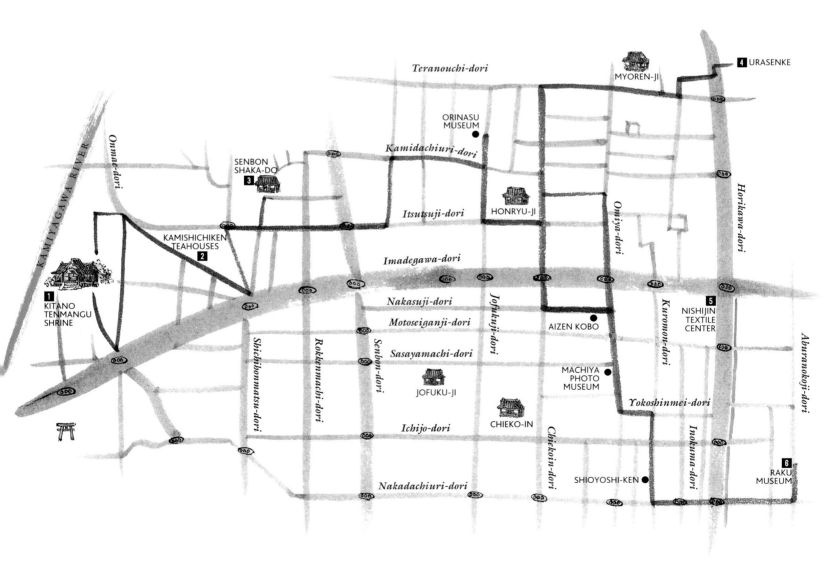

The distinctive walls of the magnificent traditional *saka-gura* warehouses of Gekkeikan, one of the oldest and the largest saké breweries in Japan, line the canal that flows through the Fushimi district in Chushojima.

For the past three hundred years, special saké brewers called *toji* have journeyed from their homes on the Japan Sea Coast every winter to do the backbreaking work of producing fine saké in Fushimi. Today only a handful of these master brewers carry on this great tradition. ▶

FUSHIMI

FOR THE BOATMEN WHO PLIED THE RIVERS between Kyoto and Osaka in the seventeenth century, Fushimi was a stop to be remembered. More than a port town, Fushimi was the home of the finest saké brewers in Japan, and so it remains today. No less than thirty-three breweries still operate in this traditional neighborhood to the south of Kyoto, including Gekkeikan, the largest saké brewery in the world.

A fifteen-minute train ride from Sanjo Station on the Keihan Line takes you to Chushojima. A short walk from the station leads you through the narrow little streets in this southernmost part of the Fushimi district to a willow-lined canal.

Here you'll find the old saké warehouses in which Gekkeikan has been producing saké for the past three hundred years. The white walls and tiled roofs of these *saka-gura* have become a symbol of this historic district and are its most distinctive architectural feature.

Gekkeikan has taken great pains to preserve its old *kura*, opening it to the public as a saké museum (closed Mondays), where one can sample great saké and learn about how it is made. In the old days, farmers from villages along the Japan Sea to the north traveled to Fushimi during the fallow winter months to become *toji*, or master saké brewers, a custom still observed at Gekkeikan each winter, though now in a largely ceremonial way.

Fushimi became the center of saké production over four centuries ago when Toyotomi

Beautifully designed labels from some of Kyoto's finest saké brewers. Horizontally from top left: Gekkeikan, Hinode-zakari (by Matsumoto Shuzo), Tamanohikari, Kizakura, Kinshi Masamune, Tomio (by Kitagawa Honke), Kinpyo (by Sanpo Shuzo), and Shochikubai (by Takara Shuzo).

Although few of the original saké warehouses remain standing in Fushimi today, Matsumoto Shuzo maintains its original buildings in elegant style.

Hideyoshi built his castle, Fushimi Momoyama Castle, on a hilltop nearby. The rivers that converged here made Fushimi a natural port, linking it with the merchants of Sakai (now part of Osaka), to the south, who could provide them with great quantities of the best rice available for saké making. Pure spring water is the key to fine saké brewing, and this was another asset Fushimi possessed.

The combination of a castle full of thirsty samurai, navigable rivers, excellent rice, and pure water contributed to making Fushimi the saké capital of Japan. Walking the streets of Fushimi from Chushojima, past the *saka-gura* of Gekkeikan in the direction of Fushimi Momoyama Station, will take you through an old market district where you'll find shops selling everything from sushi to grilled quail—and all the thirty-eight brands of locally made saké. Though many of the old shops have been replaced by modern stores, a number of hidden treasures still exist among their newer neighbors.

Like the saké this town produces, Fushimi itself has a flavor all its own—a quality the Japanese call "robust." The latticed windows and doorways lack the fragile refinement of those in central Kyoto. Instead, they are sturdier, heavier, more permanent-looking than their counterparts further north. Fushimi was a *joka-machi*, a town built at the foot of a castle, although only a replica of the original castle remains at Momoyama.

Stop for lunch at Torisei, an *izakaya*, or saké pub, which specializes in grilled chicken dishes and has a tiny shop beside the entrance that sells several brands of Fushimi saké as well as the little white-and-blue tasting cups connoisseurs use to judge the quality and color of saké.

Teradaya is another site of historic interest beside the canal at Chushojima. This traditional inn, or *ryokan*, was the scene of a famous incident in 1864 that occurred during the struggle to depose the shogunate and restore the emperor to power. One of the loyalists to the imperial court, a man named Sakamoto Ryoma, now a folk hero very much in vogue with young students of history, once stayed at Teradaya. The gouges that remain in the doorposts upstairs attest to the dramatic sword fight that ensued when Sakamoto's hideout was discovered by the shogun's troops one night in 1864. Legend has it that he was in the bath when they arrived, and escaped (in the buff) out an open window and across the rooftops to the cheers of supportive residents. Teradaya still operates as an inn, but it also opens its door daily to the many history buffs who come to Fushimi to see it.

Teradaya, an inn in Fushimi where loyalist Sakamoto Ryoma hid from soldiers of the shogun during an uprising that eventually restored Emperor Meiji to power.

On the return to Kyoto, stop at Fushimi Inari Station for a visit to one of the most extraordinary Shinto shrines in all of Japan. Fushimi Inari Taisha is one of Kyoto's oldest shrines, dating to the year 711, more than eighty years before the city was founded. The central shrine is dedicated to Princess Ugatama, the goddess of rice, also known as Inari, a deity of primary importance to what is essentially a rice culture.

Since the eighth century, the shrine has attracted hundreds of thousands of visitors each year. A square wooden measure of rice was at one time the basic unit of monetary exchange. Taxes were paid in rice, something the modern business community has not forgotten. In early February, thousands of enthusiastic businessmen arrive to toss ten-thousand-yen notes into the coffers and pray for success in the coming year.

There is no more magical place in Kyoto than the vermilion tunnel of *torii* gates that virtually covers the long, forested path to the top of the hill. Finding new *torii* among the old attests to the continued faith in the rice goddess in Fushimi. Each *torii* was donated by a merchant hoping to gain the blessings of Inari-san, as the shrine is affectionately known to the people of Kyoto. Walk up through the tunnel and explore the many smaller shrines and monuments at the top of the hill. The path wanders seemingly forever, taking you out of modern-day Japan and into its spiritual past. Feel the presence of centuries of ghosts that seem to haunt the winding stone paths and understand the depth of this city's history.

There are thousands of smaller branches of Inari shrines all over the country that can be

A magical tunnel of a "thousand" vermilion *torii* shrine gates donated by worshippers of Inari, the God of Rice, leads up the hill to sacred sites behind the main hall of Fushimi Inari Taisha.

Fushimi *ningyo* clay dolls are hand-painted by local craftspeople and sold as good-luck charms at the twelve-hundred-year-old Fushimi Inari Shrine. Doll by Tanka.

identified easily by the small stone foxes guarding their gates. Foxes are elusive animals in Japanese mythology, capable of changing shape and then vanishing in a flash.

It is said that an old man bearing a bushel of rice appeared to the great Buddhist priest Kobo Daishi at the gates of Hongan-ji temple at the start of the eighth century. Kobo Daishi (meaning "Great Teacher") is the posthumous title of the priest Kukai, who is credited with having brought Shingon Buddhism from China to Japan. When Kukai asked the old man who he was, the man replied mysteriously that he was a messenger from the rice goddess at Fushimi, then disappeared mysteriously from sight. The revered Buddhist priest ordered the construction of a major Shinto shrine at Fushimi, an example of the way the indigenous Shinto beliefs were embraced by Buddhists and of why Buddhist temples often share sacred precincts with Shinto shrines, particularly with those of beloved Inari-san.

The steps that lead up to the main shrine precincts are lined with shops selling religious objects, including charms and amulets, small natural-finish wood shrines, mirrors, and ceramic Inari foxes—all important to the practice of Shinto. Note also the gaily painted clay figurines called Fushimi *ningyo*, or Fushimi dolls, perhaps the most popular souvenir of this district. They are purchased as good luck charms rather than toys, and represent heroic characters from old legends and myths. This type of clay doll is now produced in rural areas throughout Japan, but the prototypes are said to have come from Fushimi. The road running parallel to the train tracks at the foot of the shrine is a stretch of the old Tokaido Highway system, which was the main thoroughfare linking Kyoto with Edo (now Tokyo) during the seventeenth and eighteenth centuries.

FUSHIMI　伏見

GETTING THERE: From midtown, board a train on the Keihan Main Line (Honsen) bound for Osaka and get off at Chushojima, where the walk begins (lower map). To get to the Fushimi Inari Shrine (**10**), take the Keihan Main Line (Honsen) to Fushimi Inari Station (**9**).

SUGGESTED COURSE: **1** Choken-ji → **2** Gekkeikan saké museum (Okura Kinenkan) → **3** Teradaya → **4** Kizakura Kappa Country (museum and saké) → **5** Torisei → **6** Aburacho (liquor store) → **7** Shopping street → **8** Fushimi Momoyama Station (with a replica of the castle up the hill, a 7-minute bus ride from this station) → **9** Fushimi Inari Station → **10** Fushimi Inari Taisha shrine → **11** the tunnel of orange *torii* gates to the top of the hill behind the shrine.

ARCHITECTURAL FEATURES: Thick white-plastered walls, a heavy expanse of tiled roofs of the *saké kura*, and the heavy wooden *koshi* slats over the windows of the remaining Fushimi *machiya*. The giant round balls of cryptomeria needles that hang from above the doorways of the *kura* are a symbol of the saké trade.

BEST TIME OF DAY: Leave on a morning train for Fushimi and spend the whole day wandering by the saké breweries and visiting the shrine.

BEST SEASON: Saké-brewing season in the winter months. Although it may be cold, the saké will warm you up. If you arrive in early February, you may be able to catch the wildly crowded Hatsu-Uma celebration for success in the New Year at Fushimi Inari Shrine (though it may be an even more memorable experience to walk alone at quieter times through the reddish-orange *torii* gates on the hillside).

ESTIMATED TIME: Half a day or a whole day (depending upon how much time you choose to spend exploring all the sights along the way).

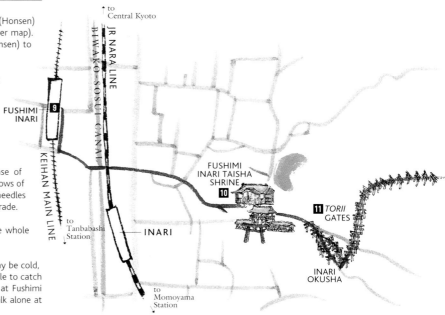

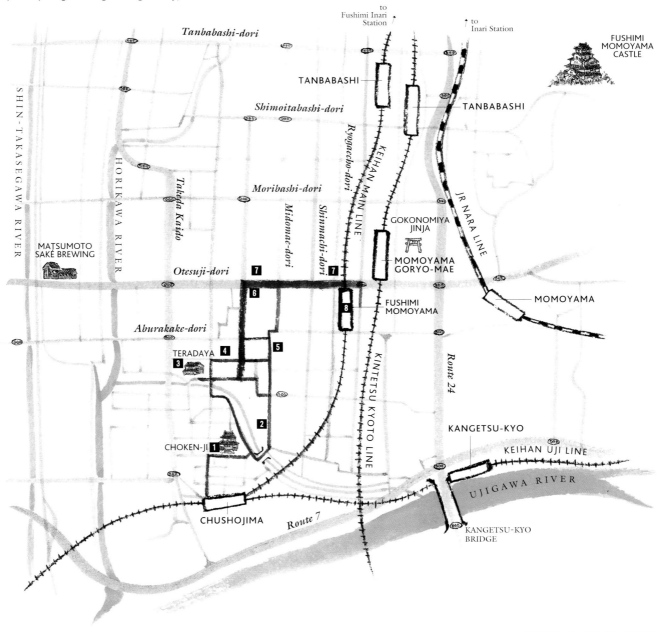

UJI 宇治

TEN MILES FROM KYOTO down a highway that was once the only road to Nara lies the quiet town of Uji, whose name has echoed in Japanese history for over twelve centuries. As one looks out over the river that flows down through Uji from the lush green hills, it is not hard to imagine court noblemen and their ladies at the height of Japan's Golden Age in the Heian period (794–1185), luxuriating at private villas here in their favorite retreat.

It was in Uji that the great court minister Fujiwara Michinaga (966–1027) chose to build his elegant summer residence. The most powerful man at court, Michinaga was also known for his poetry, his musical accomplishments, and for the magnificent building now known as the Byodo-in. Upon his death, the villa was turned into a monastery that still stands on the same

A pair of elegant bronze phoenixes, symbol of rebirth, rise proudly from both of the finials of the Byodo-in temple, arguably one of the most exquisite works of architecture created in Japanese history.

Mists hover at dawn above what may have inspired Lady Murasaki's legendary "Bridge of Dreams" across the Ujigawa river, re-creating the same melancholy atmosphere that drew Kyoto's reclusive aristocracy here centuries ago.

site after more than nine hundred years, the only example of Heian-period architecture that remains standing today.

Some believe that Michinaga was the model for the "Shining Prince" Genji in Lady Murasaki Shikibu's classic novel, *The Tale of Genji*, and that Uji was the setting in which she placed her final chapters. In real life, Murasaki had served the wife of one of Fujiwara's chief advisors. Indeed, the Uji Bridge may have been the inspiration for the Floating Bridge of Dreams of which Murasaki wrote so beautifully in the final chapter of her great novel. The last ten chapters, known as "The Uji Chapters," are set in the sad years following Genji's death, when his son, Kaoru, and grandson, Niou, play out their tragic destinies at Uji, lost in a romantic triangle with the daughters of a ruined nobleman who lives in a house beside the Ujigawa river.

The river and its Floating Bridge of Dreams are symbols of one of the novel's central themes—that life is an illusion, fraught with both great beauty and unbearable sadness. Predictable only in the certainty of death, it is a dream state between this and other worlds and incarnations, a vision which is in accordance with Buddhist traditions of the day.

The locations of significant incidents from the final chapters of this great novel are marked on the Path of History that runs along both sides of the Ujigawa river. The Tale of Genji Museum, not far from Uji Station, is a Mecca to which many ardent Japanese fans of this ageless story journey to share in *awaré*, a melancholy sense of pathos that permeates much of Japanese literature and culture—life floats along the river between this world and that.

Yet the Uji Bridge does not dissolve into history at the end of the Heian period. A century later, the aging General Minamoto Yorimasa (1104–80) of the Genji clan made his last stand here with a small band of warriors against legions of the Heike clan, defending a twelve-year-old imperial prince. Outnumbered a hundred to one, Yorimasa and his warriors went down and the prince was murdered, though his name lives in history as a hero, what scholar Ivan Morris calls an example of "the nobility of failure" appreciated by the Japanese people.

Four centuries later, the great General Toyotomi Hideyoshi stood on the Uji Bridge and drew a bucket of crystal-clear water for his tea, an event commemorated with a tea festival held each October. In a famous Kyogen play, an ancestor of the Tsuen tea family was immortalized for committing suicide in exhaustion after preparing tea for many straight days to serve Hideyoshi's thirsty troops.

Women in traditional costume pick tea in the lush green fields of Uji, purveyors of tea to the Imperial Court for centuries.

GETTING THERE: Uji is located beside the Ujigawa river less than ten miles to the southeast of Kyoto on the road that was once the only path from Nara to Kyoto. From midtown, board a train on the Keihan Main Line (Honsen) bound for Osaka, but get off midway at Chushojima. Change to the Keihan Uji Line and continue till the end of the line. From Kyoto Station, take the JR Nara Line to Uji Station. The ride takes thirty to forty minutes.

SUGGESTED COURSE: **1** Uji Bridge → **2** Omotesando (the street filled with shops leading to the temple) → **3** Byodo-in (World Cultural Heritage Site) → **4** Asagiri Bridge → **5** Asahi-yaki Pottery Center → **6** Kosho-ji temple → **7** Ujigami Jinja shrine (World Cultural Heritage Site) → **8** The Tale of Genji Museum → **9** Tsuen Tea Shop.

ARCHITECTURAL FEATURES: The Byodo-in itself is one of the most important architectural monuments in Japan, and was founded as a temple in the eleventh century. It is not known just how it has survived the many battles and fires that have destroyed the rest of the city over the centuries. Ujigami Jinja, dating from the early eleventh century, is considered the oldest extant Shinto shrine in Japan. Both these buildings are recognized as World Heritage Sites by UNESCO.

Some other landmarks include the Tsuen Tea Shop, over 330 years old, on the northeast corner of the Uji Bridge. Antique tea jars line the shelves in the interior of the main part of the shop, which has largely remained unchanged since the late seventeenth century. The wooden statue inside was carved by the famous priest Ikkyu, a friend of the seventh-generation owner of Tsuen. The white-washed walls of the shop and dark recesses of the interior offer a glimpse into a past that lives on here in the twenty-three-generation Tsuen family. In the adjoining tea shop and confectionery, have a bowl of green tea, a sweet cake, and a bowl of *sanshoku-cha soba* noodles ("three-colored tea noodles") for lunch overlooking the Ujigawa river. This shop has been selling the finest green tea for over twenty generations in the same location.

BEST SEASON: Come to Uji in the spring, when Japan's green-tea connoisseurs arrive to sample *shincha*, the year's first crop of the tender tea leaves, picked from the lush plantations, whose tidy round rows of tea plants define the rolling hillsides just outside the city. Or sit beneath the great wisteria arbor at the Byodo-in in April.

The first Sunday in October is the occasion of a major tea festival each year in celebration of the great masters of tea, who are said to have favored Uji. Cormorant fishing, done in the traditional fashion with birds roped to the fisherman, who ride in wooden flat boats by torchlight, is observed from the middle of June through September each year. The autumn color at Kosho-ji is most vibrant in early to mid-November. Call the Uji Information Center (0774–23–3334, in Japanese only) for details, or drop by for a free eight-page pamphlet in English. A four-hour English-language tour can be arranged for ¥1,000 per person. English-speaking volunteer guides can also be arranged by calling in advance (0774–22–5083).

ESTIMATED TIME: Half a day.

On the path that leads to the Byodo-in, the air is heavy with the fragrance of roasting tea leaves, wafting from the shop fronts of Uji's many fine tea shops.

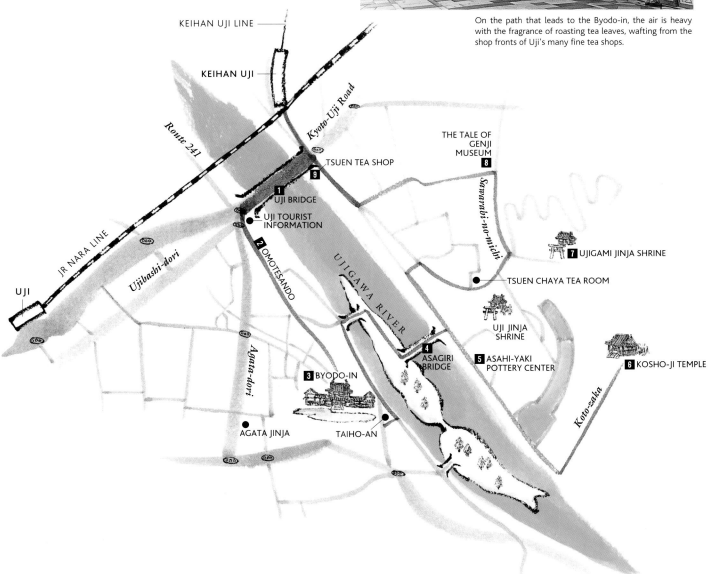

When you arrive in Uji, head first for the Byodo-in. From Uji Station on the Keihan Uji Line, walk across the bridge and up the path lined with wonderful shops old and new that offer samples of fresh-brewed green tea. Uji tea is what the emperor drinks. Stop for a refreshing cup on your way to the Byodo-in, the exquisitely constructed Buddhist temple that is depicted on the back of every ten-yen coin.

Enter the gates of the Byodo-in and walk around the pond for your first glimpse of one of the most memorable sights in all of Japan, the elegantly shaped Phoenix Hall, named for the exquisite pair of bronze phoenixes perched on the rooftop. The pair rises out of the dust of Eastern mythology just as it does in the West, promising rebirth in a better world.

Modeled after the original imperial palace at Kyoto, the "wings" on either side of the structure are marvelously decorative—what appears to be open rooms on each side in reality are not tall enough to stand up in. The proportions are a beautifully balanced ornamentation, placing art above functionality. This was the Fujiwara era after all, Japan's "Golden Age," when practicality took a back seat to the splendor of aristocratic culture.

Unlike the days of the Fujiwara, we common folk are now permitted to venture inside the Byodo-in. The great gilded Amida Buddha, carved by Jocho, one of the greatest wood sculptors in Japanese art history, is surrounded by legions of gentle *apsaras* musicians, playing here amid a vision of the Pure Promised Land. These *apsaras* are so revered that the people of Uji have built a new and elegant museum tucked away in the hillside behind the Byodo-in. Carefully restored paintings on the walls and doors depict this Buddhist paradise to which Heian people aspired. Behind the Byodo-in, a wonderfully designed museum now houses some of the temple's most remarkable treasures, which for centuries faced the elements inside this open wooden structure that has stood to everyone's wonder for nearly ten centuries.

Across the river, Ujigami Jinja, the oldest and among the most beloved of Shinto shrines, conceals itself modestly among the silent hills. The unassuming beauty of Ujigami Shrine is a hidden treasure of Uji. Dating from the tenth century, it is the oldest shrine in Japan, and all that is left of an architectural style that is at once elegant and understated.

Here, too, is Kosho-ji temple, where the great Zen priest Dogen first taught the path to a "gentleness of spirit" in the thirteenth century through a form of seated meditation known as zazen. The gardens here borrow autumn colors from the surrounding trees in mid-November, making this a setting where enlightenment seems almost within reach.

On the way is one of the only places where Asahi-yaki ceramics are still produced. The coarse, sandy, clay base and delicate, mottled pink "deer spotting" glaze pattern that characterize Asahi ware were popular with the great tea master Kobori Enshu in the seventeenth century. In Uji, the Matsubayashi family is the last of the great pottery families still working in this tradition, as they have for fourteen generations, and their small museum is another of Uji's hidden treasures.

Uji is a treasure whose people know it. Over the past decade, the township of Uji has undertaken a project that has made it a model of historic preservation in Japan. Beyond the wealth of history and the natural beauty of the setting, Uji is the home of a community of proud people who have come together in an effort to restore their historic district with dignity and a touch of panache. You have the sense that this is a living town, rather than just a tourist destination. The people have petitioned the local government to help them restore scenic paths and monuments, making a stroll through Uji a chance for a glimpse of the rapidly disappearing historical face of Japan.

The magnificent Byodo-in elegantly draped in wisteria. Sit beneath the great arbor in mid-spring and inhale the intoxicating fragrance of these delicate flowers in full bloom.

A combmaker cuts the teeth of a boxwood comb—his hands "remember" the space between.

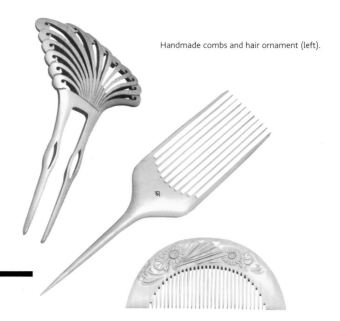

Handmade combs and hair ornament (left).

CRAFTS

ART IS NOT A THING—IT IS A WAY.

In a dimly lit tatami mat room on a narrow alley in the heart of Kyoto, a craftsman sits on the floor of his workshop in front of a low wooden bench all day long, as he has done every day of his life since he was fifteen. His father worked at this same bench and the tools that hang on the walls around him have been handed down for generations. The patterns he follows are from the worn pages of a notebook that his grandfather kept nearly seventy years ago. This man makes wooden combs.

From the cutting of the tree to the final polish, it takes ten years to produce a single *tsuge-kushi*, or boxwood comb. Only the finest wood is used to make a comb that will become a family heirloom, passed down from grandmother to mother to daughter in the years to come. The wood must be specially smoke-dried and cured for years before the craftsman cuts the piece from which the comb will be fashioned. He does not measure the teeth with rulers—his hand and eye know the distance by heart.

The crafts of Kyoto are known for their refinement and elegance. Few objects made in Kyoto display the earthy, spontaneous flavor of folk crafts from the countryside. Instead, they reflect the studied precision and delicacy of an old established society, full of pride in its sometimes cumbersome traditions and customs, and its legacy as the classical imperial city of Japan.

Starting with the gift of techniques brought from China and Korea twelve hundred years ago, the craftsmen who followed the imperial court to Kyoto in 794 began to mold and interpret these imported skills into an expression of their own. They wrought an aesthetic that valued asymmetry and simplicity by using techniques that allow the beauty of natural materials to be displayed to best advantage—understatement, subtlety, and elegance in design. All this combines with a color sense that startles the Western eye.

In the ten centuries that Kyoto was the capital, it was the center for the production of the finest arts and crafts in Japan. Kyoto was not only the home of the imperial court, it was the center of religion, the scene of the development of aesthetic pursuits like the tea ceremony, and long-term home to the performing arts of music, theater, and dance. There were royal garments to be woven; serving trays to be lacquered; Buddhist statues to be carved and gilded, tea bowls to be thrown; iron kettles to be cast; musical instruments to be fashioned; and elaborate costumes to be designed, woven, embroidered, and dyed.

During the Muromachi period (1333–1568), when craftsmanship was at its height in Kyoto, entire neighborhoods grew up around a particular craft, like the weavers and dyers of Nishijin. The guilds they formed were under the protection of neighboring temples and shrines in whose precincts open markets were held, providing craftsmen with a stable income in return for tithing.

The relationship between families within a traditional neighborhood in Kyoto was tightly bound to the craft for which it was known. Each household undertook only one step in the process. A lacquerer only applied the lacquer to a wooden tray that someone else had made. Weavers did not dye their own thread, and dyers obtained their thread from someone else. In rural districts, this division of labor was not possible. Each farmer's family made everything they needed themselves, from start to finish. The population in Kyoto, however, was large, and the finest craftsmen were attracted here to provide the imperial court and the feudal lords with finery. Traces of the complicated system of guilds that developed over the centuries and evidence of the high level of craftsmanship that was achieved can still be found in the traditional craftsmen's workshops that remain in the old neighborhoods of Kyoto today.

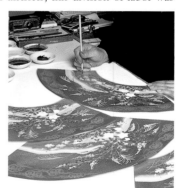

A skillful painter decorates fans.

A fan in the Kyoto style.

Applying one of many coats of lacquer.

Traditionally, dyed *yuzen* textiles were rinsed in river water.

A lacquered box.

Pottery making.

A typical example of the locally produced porcelain, known as either Kyoto ware (Kyo-yaki), Kiyomizu ware (Kiyomizu-yaki), or a combination of both terms.

A *yuzen* kimono with embroidery, Edo period.

Yuba, a Kyoto delicacy which is skimmed from steaming vats of soy milk and dried into interesting shapes, adds protein and unusual texture to soups and sauces of *shojin ryori*, the vegetarian cuisine served in many of the city's Zen temples.

CUISINE

AN ELEGANT BANQUET for a nobleman, a tea master's meticulous repast, the bare sustenance of a Zen priest, morsels to whet the appetite of a carousing samurai, simple fare for the working man—*Kyo-ryori*, or Kyoto cuisine, is an intriguing blend of a thousand years of history with as many exotic ingredients, from fresh fern greens to pickled herring to *yuba*.

Yuba is perhaps the quintessential Kyoto ingredient. Skimmed from open vats of steaming soy milk, *yuba* is served fresh with a light sauce, or dried in strips or rolls to be used later in soups and a variety of inventive ways. Almost pure protein, *yuba* is an important ingredient in Zen vegetarian cooking (as is *fu*, its glutinous wheat counterpart). The flavor is subtle, and indescribable; the texture, delicate. *Yuba* is a backdrop against which other ingredients play—the blank space that defines the culinary lines, a master's touch to a cuisine that is truly an art.

■ ■ ■

The *fusuma* door slides open . . . *s-s-s-h-u-s-h*. A maid kneels outside, bows, apologizes quietly for the intrusion. You are seated on a pillow in a tatami room overlooking a garden. The sound of water trickling into a stone basin outside has helped to wash away the day's frustrations. You have been sitting here, sipping the green tea, eating the small sweet that has gently awakened your appetite, exactly as it was intended. The first lacquered tray of morsels appears just in time.

Kaiseki promises you'll never be bored. The meal you are served depends on the precise time of year. The best chefs guarantee their guests will never receive the same meal twice. In Kyoto, a meal is to be savored by more than the palate. There is atmosphere in which to lavish, scenery to enjoy. There are gilt-edged bowls and inlaid-lacquer boxes whose craftsmanship, design, and color may also be imbibed. There are aromas brought one at a time to tantalize an appetite for the dish that follows.

Kaiseki was designed to please emperors. It was refined and perfected by tea masters with a preference for simplicity and meticulous attention to the seasons. The Chinese characters (懐石) refer to the heated stones carried to bed inside the folds of the kimono of Zen monks, just enough to take the chill from their bellies. In the later centuries, *kaiseki*, written with less aesthetic characters (会席), became

Kyoto confectioneries, such as Tsuruya Yoshinobu, are famous throughout Japan for their delicate flavors and seasonal shapes.

Kaiseki, Japan's elegant haute cuisine, is served in a series of carefully designed courses, whose flavors, colors, and textures complement each other. Variety and seasonal appropriateness are apparent in the careful selection of tableware, which also depends on the season, the occasion, and the host's knowledge of the guest's special tastes. Here, the master of Kinmata Ryokan presents a course in elegant glass vessels.

hors d'oeuvres served with saké for the merchant class out for a night of pleasure in the geisha houses of Gion. No matter what the occasion, Kyoto-style *kaiseki* places importance on seasonal ingredients, whose flavor is to be enhanced gently, never to be overwhelmed by heavy spices or elaborate sauces. It is intended to be served graciously, enjoyed leisurely, and appreciated attentively. (Today, a *kaiseki* meal can be extremely costly, but it is an experience that does not have to be missed. For a person on a limited budget, a *kaiseki bento*, the "box lunch" supreme, will provide a delightful sampler of this magnificent cuisine.)

But Kyoto was more than aristocrats and playboys. The vast majority of people were farmers, shopkeepers, and craftsmen who never got near a *kaiseki* meal. Kyoto was a landlocked city, a two-day trek over the mountains to the sea. Fish had to be salted or pickled to be carried that far on foot by peddlers. Even vegetables had to be pickled to save them from perishing in the hot, sticky summers. The people's cuisine of Kyoto was far from exotic. A bowl of barley rice, a few pickled vegetables, a bowl of miso soup—a bite of fish when times were good—and a cup of the plainest tea; humble fare, often vegetarian, as much of the population was Buddhist.

Shojin-ryori, Zen-style cooking, served in temples and vegetarian restaurants today, turned the simple sustenance of Buddhist priests—vegetables, rice, and soybeans—into a creative and interesting cuisine that is apparent in every aspect of Japanese cooking.

The cuisine that the painstaking monks evolved explored every imaginable use of its simple ingredients, especially of soybeans—a hundred ways to serve miso, soy sauce, tofu, and *yuba*, all rich in protein. The same attention to visual beauty that other forms of *Kyo-ryori* possess is found in *shojin-ryori*, though not to such a lavish degree. Nothing should be wasted, and rather than costly porcelain, the monks each had their own stack of bowls, one fitting inside the other, wiped clean by the monk himself when the meal had been thankfully consumed.

The dimensions of Kyoto cuisine reflect the seasons and sensibilities of all the townspeople—from priest to bon vivant, from nobility to peasants.

Tofu ryori, a staple of the Zen vegetarian diet, is featured at a number of Kyoto restaurants, which are known for their tendency to specialize. This is tofu as you will never find it outside of Japan.

The essence of the tea ceremony—the thoughtful preparation of a simple bowl of whisked green tea shared in a quiet moment with a friend. Nothing more, nothing less.

TEA CEREMONY

SABI, THE QUIET DIGNITY age alone can bestow—the touch of the blue-green patina time etches on bronze, the yellowed borders of a paper scroll that has been unwrapped, admired, and put away safely a thousand times by a thousand careful hands. *Wabi,* the unpretentious beauty of an old ceramic bowl from the kilns of some anonymous country potter gone a hundred years—the humility poverty instills, a rustic simplicity, wild flowers, bamboo, water, and stone. This is the spirit of *sado,* the tea ceremony: a simple bowl of tea, a meal shared with friends—thoughtfully, deliberately, savoring the moment.

The practice of ceremonial tea was originally brought to Japan from China, but the basic philosophy fit the Japanese people like a psychic glove. Perhaps that is why it is still so much alive in Japan today, when many other traditional cultural pursuits seem to have worn thin.

The tea ceremony has left its mark on almost every aspect of life in Japan, from arts and crafts to cuisine, from social customs to psychology. The impact of *sado* is to be found everywhere in Japan—in the way houses are built, in the food people eat, even in relationships between friends—and nowhere more so than in the old neighborhoods of Kyoto.

Though *sado* was originally a pastime enjoyed exclusively by members of the aristocracy, it was the merchant class, with its aspirations to rival the upper classes, which eventually brought the aesthetics of tea ceremony into the mainstream of Japanese society in the seventeenth and eighteenth centuries.

Few of the traditional merchant homes of Kyoto are without a formal tea room, based on the original four-and-a-half–tatami mat tea room built in the fifteenth century by shogun Ashikaga Yoshimasa at his villa, now known as Ginkaku-ji, the Temple of the Silver Pavilion. This tea room became the standard, not only for other tea rooms, but for Japanese architecture as a whole.

The proportions, the natural materials, the use of light and shadow are all aesthetic considerations inspired by the tea ceremony. The *zashiki,* the formal guest room of a traditional home, always had a special alcove in which a hanging scroll, a flower arrangement, and perhaps a treasured family possession were placed.

Not only interior, but exterior features of homes in Kyoto show the influence of tea. Even the smallest *machiya* had an interior garden, though some consist of but a few carefully placed rocks, a stand of bamboo, and a stone water basin in an open-air niche the size of a hall closet. The *tsubo-niwa,* a special feature of the *machiya* of Kyoto, are often no bigger than a large ceramic crock (*tsubo*). As in the classic tea room, no home is without a touch of nature, however small, even in the midst of a crowded city.

The waterbasin of the tea house Kankyu-an on the grounds of Mushanokoji-senke, headquarters of one the great schools of *chanoyu,* the tea ceremony.

Iho-an, a thatched tea hut at Kodai-ji temple, exemplifies an exquisite harmony of natural beauty and fine craftsmanship in a meticulously tended garden setting.

Entering the home of a prosperous merchant family in anticipation of finding two or perhaps three exquisite gardens tucked within its recesses, away from public view, is a delightful prospect. The somber, heavily slatted façades of these homes conceal the wealth and tastes of their owners from ordinary passersby. In poorer neighborhoods, areas that once housed the servants and employees of wealthy merchants, the presence of nature can be seen in the carefully tended shelves laden with potted chrysanthemums, morning glories, and bonsai clinging to the very edge of the street. The flowers displayed outside these modest dwellings announce the changing seasons. Every miniature pine and azalea is snipped and trimmed with the care, patience, and humble dedication even a tea master would admire.

A thousand paper lanterns light up the night during Yoiyama, an evening celebration that leads up to the world's oldest continuously celebrated urban festival, Gion Matsuri.

FESTIVALS

A SMALL, WHITE-FACED BOY, teeth blackened, lips scarlet, robed in costly brocade, crowned with a golden phoenix, will ride this year—as he has since the tenth century—from Yasaka Jinja shrine through the streets of Kyoto to perform a spiritual rite in the name of the common people. He is the *chigo*, the boy chosen this year from among the merchant families in central Kyoto as a messenger of Susano-o, the Shinto god to whom this fantastic festival, Gion Matsuri, is dedicated.

The *chigo* has been prepared for this task for an entire year—trained in the complicated rituals he will need to perform. After weeks of spe-

cial purification ceremonies, during which he lives in pampered isolation from contaminating influences (such as the presence of women), the *chigo* is carried atop the lead float, the *naginata*, where he must cut the rope that marks the start of the procession that takes place on July 17. Failure to sever the rope with one stroke of the sword is bad luck and a dishonor to his family name forever—a huge responsibility for a child of ten.

For over eleven centuries, Gion Matsuri has filled the humid days of July in Kyoto with energy. A full month of ritual and ceremony, highlighted by several nights of celebration leading up to a spectacular procession through the center of the city, allows one to forget the heat of summer—even the passage of time.

Gion Matsuri has always belonged to the people. It originated in a plea to the gods to stop a plague that swept the capital in the ninth century. Sixty-six halberds representing the sixty-six provinces of old Japan were offered by Emperor Seiwa to appease the angry gods who were thought to have inflicted the disastrous epidemic. When the plague miraculously abated, it was decreed that a procession would be held annually in thanksgiving, and to assure that no such horror would ever again befall the city. The festival is conducted under the auspices of Yasaka Jinja, or Gion-sha, as the shrine is locally known because of its location in the heart of the Gion district.

Over the turbulent centuries of civil war that marked the middle ages in Japan, the citizens themselves took on the responsibility for the festival. By the Edo period (1600–1868), members of the rising merchant class had begun to use the festival as a means of asserting their newly gained wealth and power in a feudalistic society that had relegated them to the lowest rank. The floats, called *yama* and *hoko*, were adorned with the finest tapestries and treasures, some of which were obtained from European traders with whom the merchants of Kyoto conducted their prosperous ventures.

Having one's ten-year-old son selected the *chigo* of Gion Matsuri is one of the greatest honors a Kyoto merchant family can have. He rides the lead float as a messenger to the town gods, cutting the rope that starts the parade every year in this thousand-year-old festival.

In the Kyokusui no utage Festival at Jonangu Shrine, Fushimi, men and women in silk brocade robes reminiscent of those worn in the Heian period (794–1185) carry on the elegant aristocratic custom of composing poetry beside a stream—each poet adding his or her verse to a passing saké cup as it floats by.

The cultural significance of Gion Matsuri, particularly to the people of Kyoto, lies not only in the festival's historical continuity, but also in its expression of the irrepressible nature of the common people. Throughout feudal times and amidst a rigidly structured class system, Gion Matsuri was always a rallying point for the populace of Kyoto.

Today, visitors from all over the world come to watch the July 17 procession and marvel at the splendor of the thirty-one floats as they pass by, one after another, their giant wooden wheels now facing asphalt pavement, their halberds challenging power lines on high.

Matsuri, the word for festival in Japanese, comes from the word *matsuru*, which means to offer prayer. Gion Matsuri, like most of the other festivals in Japan, has its roots in religion. It is one of the *goryo-e* festivals, which originated as a means of appeasing the gods, who were thought to cause fires, floods, and earthquakes if not sufficiently placated.

There are over two thousand shrines and temples in Kyoto, each one an integral part of the life of the neighborhood in which it stands. The people are responsible for the care of their local shrine, and it is they who carry on its traditional ceremonies and festivals.

There are countless festivals held in Kyoto each year—some that attract thousands, some attended only by the neighborhood children. Among the largest are Jidai Matsuri, Aoi Matsuri, Gozan Okuri-bi, and Kurama Hi-matsuri.

The smallest of all—Jizobon—is a summer festival in honor the Buddhist deity Jizo, special guardian of children. During Jizobon, people decorate a little shrine to Jizo in every Kyoto neighborhood, and their children carry the portable shrine through the streets to pay homage. These shrines are tended year-round by the women of every neighborhood, each of whom takes a turn cleaning and offering flowers. Once a year in the midst of the heat of August, the little ones gather for Jizobon to play games and vie for prized plastic baubles on mats spread out in front of the neighborhood shrine, while their grandparents look on dotingly and sip cold barley tea. Of all the grand festivals celebrated in this old city, the importance of religion as a focal point for community spirit in the traditional neighborhoods of Kyoto can be seen most clearly in simple neighborhood festivals like these.

Kurama Hi-matsuri is Kyoto's most vibrant festival, with men carrying huge straw torches down the hillside and through the streets to the excited shrieks of thousands of onlookers each year.

TRAVEL INFORMATION
THE KYOTO TOURIST INFORMATION CENTER

People ask me if there is enough to do in Kyoto to keep them here for more than three days. The fact is that there are enough wonderful gardens, museums, galleries, workshops, temples, shrines, shops, and restaurants in Kyoto to keep a person busy for three years. They kept me busy for eighteen.

The fastest way to get the information you need is to call 075–371–0480 or 371–5649 or, better yet, visit the Kyoto Tourist Information Center (TIC) on the ground floor of the Kyoto Tower Building on Karasuma-dori across the street from the station. (Open from 9 A.M. to 5 P.M., Monday through Friday; from 9 A.M. to noon on Saturdays.) No matter what you are interested in seeing, studying, tasting, visiting, or watching, you can get help in both English and French at the TIC. (Ask about their volunteer guide service.)

TRANSPORTATION

Kyoto has buses, trains, subways, and an abundant supply of taxis. Because of the unpredictability of signs or instructions in English, it is often wise to call the TIC for information on the fastest, most economical way to get where you want to go. Maps are also available free of charge at the TIC.

Taxis are a reliable and time-saving alternative for those with a limited schedule, and not unreasonably priced, particularly if shared. The shiny black MK Taxi Company has some English-speaking telephone operators (075–721–4141) and, by request, excellent (though expensive) tours with English-speaking driver-guides (075–721–2237).

Bicycle rentals are available, but traffic is hectic on most of the main streets. Check with the TIC for rental-shop locations, or pick up a free copy of the *Kyoto Visitors' Guide*, available at most hotels.

Either Kyoto Station or the centrally located Sanjo Keihan Station are public transportation hubs for trains, buses, and the impeccably clean subway system. Taxi directions have been provided in Japanese and English under each of the different historic neighborhood sections in this book. Once you have arrived in the vicinity of one of the seven districts, see it on foot. One very important thing to remember is your feet. Wear comfortable, well-broken-in shoes, and don't forget that in most Japanese restaurants, homes, and inns you will have to take them off—hence, the popularity of slip-on shoes in Japan.

ENGLISH-LANGUAGE BOOKS

For maps, guidebooks, and books in English on everything from making sushi to collecting swords, visit Maruzen Book Store on Kawaramachi street between Shijo-dori and Sanjo-dori. Look for monthly magazines like *Kansai Time Out* and *Kyoto Journal* for up-to-date information on local exhibitions, festivals, and other cultural events. *Kyoto Visitors' Guide*, a free monthly information magazine, is available at the TIC and at most major hotels.

CREDITS

The publishers would like to thank the following people, groups, and organizations for graciously consenting to the use of the photographs, illustrations, and other additional material for this volume.

Byodo-in temple, pp. 54–55
Fujimoto Kempachi, photographer of Ninsei vase, pp. 14 & 15
Fukuoka Art Museum, Ninsei vase, pp. 14 & 15
Gekkeikan, permission to reproduce Mizuno's photograph, p. 49
Gion Festival Floats Association, permission to reproduce Mizuno's photographs:
    Hakurakuten-yama Hozonkai, p. 66 (top); Naginata-hoko Hozonkai, p. 66 (bottom); Tsuki-hoko Hozonkai, p. 3 (top).
Japan Traditional Craft Center, p. 60 (bottom)
Kyoto City Government (City Planning Bureau), line drawings, pp. 5, 12, 23, 28, 37
Kyoto City Government (Industrial Affairs and Tourism Bureau), from *Kyo: Saijiki*, pp. 14 (bottom right), 61 (bottom)
Kyoto Dento Kogei Kyogikai (Kyoto Traditional Handicraft Council), pp. 60 (comb-maker; combs & hair ornament, fan maker), 61 (top left)
Kyoto National Museum, pp. 42 (left), 44 (right)
Kyoto Sensu Uchiwa Shoko Kyodo Kumiai (fans commerce and industry cooperative), p. 60, (center)
Kyoto Shikkikogei Kyodo Kumiai (lacquer craft cooperative), p. 61 (top)
Kyoto Soshohin Saiho Zakka Kumiai (accessories, sewing articles cooperative), p. 60 (top)
Kyoto Tojiki Kyodo Kumiai Rengokai/JCC Inc., p. 14 (bottom left & center)
Minamiza, p. 25 (top)
Mizuno Kayu, machiya plan, p. 6 (top)
Morimoto Kazari Kanagu, cart, decorated metalwork, p. 68
National Museum of Japanese History, p. 61 (bottom right)
Suntory Museum of Art, endpapers, p. 41
Tokyo National Museum, pp. 46 (bottom), 61 (lacquerware box)

ACKNOWLEDGMENTS

This second edition of *Kyoto: Seven Paths to the Heart of the City* owes much to my editor, Barry Lancet, at Kodansha International. Barry's efforts have resurrected a "lost edition" and brought it back to light. Special thanks to Ayako Akaogi for her extensive work with the photographs and maps, and to designer Kazuhiko Miki for sculpting the images and words into the book you hold in your hand. Many thanks also to Joseph Cronin, who painstakingly walked each of the old paths again, checking for new "developments" and finding some wonderful hidden side roads in the process. Thanks to my husband, Stephen Futscher, for the long hours putting the manuscript in order and revising all the maps.

The original research for this book was assisted by a number of individuals in Kyoto, past and present, including Hiroo Kinoshita and Mitsuhiro Nishiguchi, Professor Yasuo Kitazawa, Dr. Claire Gallian, and many others. Noriko Kasuya at the Kyoto City Office has been very helpful in keeping my ties with Kyoto strong. Thank you also to Mitsumura Suiko Publishing Company, which printed the original edition and permitted this new version to be brought back to life in a new form.

Special thanks go to master photographer Katsuhiko Mizuno, whose wonderful photographs have added so much to these pages. His love of the weaving district of Nishijin and of the *Kyo-machiya* in which he lives and works greatly aids the movement to preserve them. His photographs of Kyoto keep the spirit of the city alive.

Finally, my thanks go to those in Kyoto who have kept up the struggle against all odds to keep some of the traditional quality of the old Kyoto neighborhoods alive. Not only has their commitment been instrumental in restoring many of the old wooden *machiya*, but it has also demonstrated again the significance their beloved city has as a symbol of the possibility of a strong community life in a crowded urban environment.

きょうと
京都
KYOTO: Seven Paths to the Heart of the City

2002 年 9 月 13 日　第 1 刷発行

著　者　ダイアン・ダーストン	印刷所　凸版印刷株式会社
撮影者　水野克比吉	製本所　株式会社　国宝社
発行者　畑野文夫	
発行所　講談社インターナショナル株式会社	

〒112-8652 東京都文京区音羽 1-17-14
電話　03-3944-6493（編集部）
　　　03-3944-6492（営業部・業務部）
ホームページ　http://www.kodansha-intl.co.jp

落丁本・乱丁本は、小社業務部宛にお送りください。送料小社負担にてお取替えします。なお、この本についてのお問い合わせは、編集部宛にお願いいたします。本書の無断複写（コピー）、転載は著作権法の例外を除き、禁じられています。

定価はカバーに表示してあります。